A CHURCH AT RISK

A CHURCH AT RISK

The Encroachment of American Culture Upon the Church

William W. Dean

FRANCIS ASBURY PRESS
of Zondervan Publishing House
Grand Rapids, Michigan

Francis Asbury Press is an imprint of Zondervan Publishing House,
1415 Lake Drive, S.E., Grand Rapids, Michigan 49506.

Library of Congress Cataloging in Publication Data

Dean, William Walter.
    A church at risk : the encroachment of American culture upon the church /
William W. Dean.
        p.   cm.
    ISBN 0-310-75441-0
    1. Bible. N.T. Hebrews–Devotional literature. 2. Church-Biblical teach-
ing. 3. Christian life–Methodist authors.
    I. Title.
    BS2775.4.D33   1990
    227'. 8706–dc20   89-38050
                                                                                  CIP

Edited by Robert D. Wood

Printed in the United States of America

90   91   92   93   94   95 / PP / 10   9   8   7   6   5   4   3   2   1

To my wife

Joan

*whose encouragement was essential
to the preparation of this book
and to the shared ministry
out of which it grew*

CONTENTS

FOREWORD

One does not have to be a theologian to recognize that the Christian community today, especially in the affluent Western world, is in trouble. Despite all the talk about church growth, little is happening that compels the watching world to take seriously our witness. We go through the accepted forms of religious devotion, of course, but there is little joy in it; somehow the vibrance of living faith has leaked out.

Such a situation cannot continue indefinitely. There comes a time when either we must experience renewal or inevitably there will be judgment. We may be nearer that point now than we think.

Dr. William Dean is mindful of this danger. Using passages in Hebrews as a reference, he comes to grips with basic issues that must be confronted in the life of the church.

The author pulls no punches. This is hard-hitting stuff. Not the kind of reading one will find entertaining while reclining in a cushioned chair eating chocolates.

Yet in these practical expositions of Scripture, he brings us to see the triumph of grace that can be experienced by everyone truly seeking first the kingdom of God.

We need more of this. That's why I commend this book to you. It cuts through the nice talk, and brings us to see the glorious calling to follow Jesus.

Robert E. Coleman
Trinity Evangelical Divinity School
Deerfield, Illinois

PREFACE

I am a historian by training and a minister by calling. I have approached this study with a great deal of trepidation because of the theological issues involved. But I have sought to explore the doctrine of the church in the epistle to the Hebrews with both feet firmly planted in the historical realities of the first century—and of the twentieth.

This is not a commentary on the epistle. Rather, as a historian, I have used the letter to explore the author's understanding of the church. And also as a historian, I have tried to explain simply and directly its implications for modern Christians.

Luke gave us a vibrant account of the early church in action. Paul gave us a theological foundation for the existence of the church. But this brother (whose identity no one knows) gave us insight into the meaning of the church that is sharp and urgent because of the dangers that he saw threatening it. This aspect of the epistle has rarely been developed or even acknowledged. Our circumstances are widely different as we approach the twenty-first century, but American Christianity stands at risk in similar straits.

Again, this is not a commentary. Many passages, themes, and ideas important to the author I have chosen not to treat. However, I urge you to read the passages quoted from Hebrews, which form the foundations of the chapters, and to keep your Bible open for ready reference. Themes are introduced and explored as they appear in the epistle, except in a few cases where related ideas arise from different paragraphs or chapters.

Three interrelated themes provide the framework of this study:

First and most prominent, the meaning of *companionship with God our Father*. Because they were about to settle for something far less than God intended, the writer of the epistle was concerned that the Hebrew Christians should understand how God has chosen to relate to us.

Second, the *fellowship of the church*. Our author was concerned about the nature of the relationships that existed between and among believers. In fact, he saw that relations with God and with fellow believers were so interdependent that the loss of either destroyed both.

Third, the importance of our *responsiveness to the grace of God*. This Hebrew pastor understood the responsibility that men and women have to listen and respond to God's initiatives. All relationships are created and energized by God, but he does not and will not force a relationship on anyone.

Any study worthy of the label "Bible study" must not only inform our minds but also lead us into the presence of the God who seeks our companionship. The hymns that I have placed at the ends of chapters are some of my favorites. But they are more, much more: they are prayers of response. I trust that this study will encourage you to learn—and worship.

William W. Dean
Forest City, North Carolina
September 1, 1989

1

IN THE DEATH GRIP OF COMPLACENCY

Hebrews 1:1–2:4

Americans are fascinated by the British royal family. I often look over the magazine racks in the supermarket checkout lanes, and rarely are Prince Charles or Princess Diana missing from the cover or headlines of at least one issue. We have read the details of their storybook wedding in St. Paul's Cathedral, the birth of their children, their skiing expeditions, and—of course—their marital spats. When Charles and Di visit America (to say nothing of when the queen comes) they are treated, well, royally! We are fascinated by them.

While my family and I were living in northern England several years ago, we decided that our sons, then four and seven, needed to see the sights in London. The first order of business was a visit to Buckingham Palace for the changing of the guard. While we were jostling for a position outside the imposing iron fence around the palace, we began to listen to the people near us. The accents were strangely familiar. We heard Southerners and Easterners and Westerners, but we didn't hear a single British accent! Most of the ardent admirers and fans at the gates of Buckingham Palace were Americans. What use do we have with all the pomp and circumstance that goes with royalty? Yet we are fascinated with it.

There is a curious anomaly in this sentimental attachment. For all our interest, the royal family means nothing to us so far as an allegiance is concerned; we do not regard them as our spokespersons; we do not seek their opinions; we are not especially interested in their points of view on topics of the day. We certainly have no desire that the Windsors should again rule over us. (George III was Charles' great-great-great-great-great-grandfather.)

WE MUST TAKE JESUS SERIOUSLY

The writer of the letter to the Hebrews was deeply concerned that his fellow Christians were in great danger: they no longer took Jesus seriously. These Hebrew Christians had suffered much for their faith in Christ as Messiah. They were well aware of the price the previous generation—their fathers and mothers—had paid. But those memories were not enough to protect them from mortal danger.

The Hebrew epistle is not addressed to the pagan world of the first century. The unnamed author was not writing to sinners, the moral reprobates in gutters and palaces. He was not even writing to sincere Jews who still held to the old covenant. He wrote to a group who called themselves followers of Jesus the Christ. And blazed in flaming words from beginning to end is this warning: Take Jesus seriously!

I must digress a moment here to let you in on a very personal struggle I have faced. I entered the ministry with adequate Bible training. I was something of a would-be intellectual, I suppose; I marvel at the patience and grace demonstrated by members of my first congregation. But after six years of preaching and teaching the Scriptures as best I could, I left the ministry—forever, I thought at the time. My frustration and disillusionment stemmed partly from my own unreasonable expectations, but also partly from the plain fact that in six years of sincere work in the ministry, I had accomplished little that was of spiritual value. I had seen a few converts, a few new members, a remodeled building, but so little when compared with the needs I felt.

I tried new and innovative programs; I led studies on spiritual gifts; I organized leadership retreats and encouraged church leaders to attend seminars. I became convinced that no one, certainly not members of the congregation, really took me seriously. But I was young and green, and I tried to make allowances for that. What really cut the foundations from under me was an unarticulated suspicion that hovered over me like an invisible yet smothering, sinister presence: no one took the Bible seriously either! If the preaching of the Word made no difference, why waste my time? I resigned, returned to graduate school, and intended to become a teacher.

God had other plans, however, and he led me back into the pastoral ministry by one of his circuitous paths of grace. But the nagging suspicion has been transmuted into conviction. I understand the burden of our Hebrew colleague far more deeply than I can express in words. The awful danger, the agonizing need, the terrible indictment that falls on American Christians today is the glaring truth that we don't take Jesus seriously at all. God help us.

Who is Jesus? For many who frequent our services weekly, he is a remote figure whom we have dug out of dusty volumes of history. He is distant and far away, an image from a different time, a different age, a different culture and language—almost a different world. He is so remote that he has nothing to do with anything important so far as this present world is concerned. Too many Christians give mental assent to the reality of God in Christ, but the world of work and the world of faith are light years apart. God is distant, oh, so distant, a tantalizing yet insubstantial phantom on the edges of consciousness.

For some, Jesus is simply a guide, a good moral teacher who showed the world the way to live happily. He is a personal guru who teaches us to treat others as we would be treated; to love our neighbors as we love ourselves; to do good to our enemies; to be civil, and kind, and generous. Christians know this conventional Jesus because they learned of him as children in Sunday school and in bedtime stories. Their "faith" is a Christian orientation that was woven into their personalities by church-going parents. But beyond the conventional practice of sitting in the pew, Jesus seldom gets a second thought.

For a few, Jesus was a martyr who, years ago, laid down his life for what he believed to be the truth. He was a good man, who loved his fellowman, who died for truth, justice, and righteousness. He was an idealist and a radical, a man of courage who refused to play the religious games of status and influence. He deserves to be imitated and copied as reformers tackle the thorny social and economic problems of our day. But a living, contemporary Companion? No way!

I know very well that American evangelicals will declare that Jesus is more—much more—than a guide, or teacher, or hero. We will declare with passion that he is the Son of God, the Savior of the world, the coming King. We put him on our stationery, our checks, our lapels, our datebooks, our Christmas cards, and our bumper stickers. But most of us do not take seriously the direct implications of that declaration. If Jesus Christ is the Son of God, if he is who he claimed to be, then to call him Lord is an awesome statement. The second sentence of the letter to the Hebrews is as plain as words can make it: "The Son is the radiance of God's glory, and the exact representation [KJV says *image*] of his being" (1:3). In other words, when Jesus Christ came into this world, he came as a man, and yet he came as God. Up to that point, through all the ages since creation, people could have said, "Where is God? I have never seen God. I don't understand God. What does God require of me?" Now, God has come to us in Jesus Christ. When we say that Jesus Christ is Lord, that he is the Son of God, we are saying that God has walked among us.

Jesus did not come merely with words and professions. He came with the power of God (2:4). No other one who ever lived was visited by astrologers from a thousand miles away looking for the king of the Jews. No other birth has ever been announced by angels in the skies. No one who ever lived has been able to turn water into wine with a word, has been able to give sight to a Bartimaeus or life to a Lazarus. This is Jesus, who came with the power of God, with the glory of God, with the nature of God, revealing to us who God is.

When we say that Jesus Christ is Lord, that he is the Son of God, we are saying that Jesus has revealed to us all we need to know about God's requirements and provision. Our acknowledgment of that revelation also lays on us a personal and engrossing responsibility. If we profess to be Christian, it is time to take Jesus seriously.

A. W. Tozer has described our American Christian attitude in a stunning paragraph.

> God is admitted only by man's sufferance. He is treated as visiting royalty in a democratic country. Everyone takes His name upon his lips and (especially at certain seasons) He is feted and celebrated and hymned. But behind all this flattery men hold firmly to their right of self-determination. As long as man is allowed to play host he will honor God with his attention, but always He must remain a guest and never seek to be Lord. Man will have it understood that this is his world; he will make its laws and decide how it shall be run. God is permitted to decide nothing. Man bows to Him and as he bows, manages with difficulty to conceal the crown upon his own head.[1]

The writer of Hebrews moves quickly into the burden of his heart. In four verses he summarizes the gospel of Jesus Christ. Then follow ten verses of supporting quotations from various Old Testament passages, emphasizing the place that Jesus holds in the spiritual universe. If Jesus is God, if he is enthroned as King of kings, if we are to face him as our Judge, then pay attention!

Twice in 2:1–3 the idea of *neglect* appears. First, there is the warning concerning "drifting away," and, second, the conditional verb "if we ignore." Let's look closely at each of these phrases. Remember, this is addressed to Christian believers.

THE NEGLECT FROM COMPLACENCY

Perhaps we can best understand the meaning of the first phrase through a homemade parable. Once there were two young men named Andrew and Jeremy. They were adventurous and confident. They decided to canoe down an unfamiliar river. It would be a long and arduous trip, but they were no strangers to canoeing. Being sensible young men, they gathered all the information they could find about the river. They found maps and talked to others who had canoed there.

From every source they were warned repeatedly, and in strongest terms, about one impassable stretch of white water. A portage would be necessary. Rapids and falls, if not avoided, meant certain death. Even the map the boys obtained from the forest ranger bore the warning: "This stretch is impassable." Also marked on the map were outstanding landmarks so that canoers would have no difficulty in knowing when to leave the river. The mapmaker had spared no pains to be sure that no one would be surprised by the dangerous rapids.

So with the warnings and with the map, Andrew and Jeremy started out. There was just enough current so that the boys could paddle along without working too hard. They were having a grand time. The farther they went, the easier it seemed to get. They kept the map there in front of them, and watched for the landmarks. From time to time they had to duck under overhanging branches; they floated down the river with everything going perfectly. No spills, no water in the canoe, no surprises, and no mistakes.

In the distance they began to hear a roar that gradually grew louder, but things were going so well that the boys decided that they still had plenty of time before putting in to shore. The roar grew louder still, and the current picked up. The landmarks passed one by one, and Andrew and Jeremy began to look for a good spot to get out, but not until the last possible minute. They rounded a bend, and suddenly the current grabbed the canoe as if it were a floating leaf. The roar had become deafening. Instantly, both boys knew that this was it and began to paddle furiously toward a point of land at the next bend. The harder they paddled, the faster the current whisked them on. As they swept around the point, paddling furiously, they discovered that they had waited too long.

That is the kind of neglect that theatens Christians. It is not that we go out and commit heinous crime, that we blatantly thumb our noses at God and walk away. It is simply that we get caught in the current of life in this world, and we are lost.

Neglect! The neglect of complacency; the neglect of drifting along with the flow. We have our map, and we know the warnings; we know what is at stake, but we are not going to get really serious about it until the last possible moment.

And what happens? We obey him when it is convenient. We listen to those commands that are most compatible with our comfort and selfishness. We rely on our middle-class morality and our frequent contact with the church for our acceptance with God. It is a horrid thought, repulsive to our modern minds, that good, though nominal, Christians are in eternal danger—these folks who attend church, pay their tithes, and profess to have had a religious experience somewhere in the past. But if that is not the case, then the entire book of Hebrews is a pointless exercise.

THE NEGLECT FROM DISDAIN

The second neglect is a different matter altogether. This phrase translated "if we ignore" is used only one other time in the New Testament, in the parable Jesus told about the king who prepared a wedding banquet for his son. Those invited "paid no attention" to the summons. The word Matthew uses is the same as that which here is translated "ignore" (Matt. 22:5).

This is neglect resulting not from complacency nor from comfort but from contempt. These men thumbed their noses at this invitation. They flaunted it. One said, "I have bought a team of oxen, and I must go and try them out." Another said, "I have bought property, and I must go and look at it. Another said, "I have married a wife, and I can't come" (Lk. 14:16–21).

They flouted, with excuses, the invitation of the king. This was not merely passing up an opportunity. We would not spurn an invitation to the home of a friend. If we were invited to dinner, we would do everything we could to go. Even if we received an invitation that we did not wish to accept, we would at least try to turn it down courteously. But here were those who rejected the invitation of the king, and walked away to their own destruction.

GOD INVITES US TO BE HIS COMPANIONS

The clear invitation of sacred Scripture is God's personal call to every believer to a life of discipleship, to walk with Jesus day by day in the fellowship of his church. That means that we put him first in our lives, the lives of our families, in our business relationships, in our work, our home life, in our priorities, in the use of our money. He calls us to walk in the company of the King of the universe; to be his friend; to have a relationship with him.

God is serious about this business of being Lord. He sent Jesus into our world to live and to die. He died to be Lord. He does not save those who do not allow him to be Lord of their lives. He will be Savior *and* Lord, or he will be neither Savior nor Lord. We can't have it both ways. We cannot run our own lives and make our own decisions, with a take-it-or-leave-it attitude toward God.

We can accept God's judgment against disdain, and we are disturbed when we see others show contempt toward eternal values. But our Hebrew author warns that neglect in any form is dangerous. Whether we simply coast along in complacency or whether we thumb our noses at God's invitation, it amounts to the same thing. We could miss eternal life.

For many Christians, the implications of that last paragraph border on heresy. We are saved solely by the grace of God through faith in Jesus Christ. Nothing we can do merits favor with God: not Bible study, not prayer, not church attendance, not witnessing, not anything. Period. I do believe and teach that with all my heart. But I also find that God's grace demands a response from me. If there is no response, then there is no salvation. If God programmed human response, the Scriptures state that all would then be saved (2 Peter 3:9). Since God's grace is constantly flowing into our lives, we must continue to be responsive to God. And in that responsiveness is the companionship that God wants to have with every believer.

The themes of grace, responsibility, and fellowship with God and other believers are interwoven throughout this epistle.

Let us together ask the Father to enlighten us as we follow them.

O Master, let me walk with thee
In lowly paths of service free;
    Tell me thy secret; help me bear
The strain of toil, the fret of care.

Help me the slow of heart to move
By some clear, winning word of love;
    Teach me the wayward feet to stay,
And guide them in the homeward way.

Teach me thy patience; still with thee
In closer, dearer company,
    In work that keeps faith sweet and strong,
In trust that triumphs over wrong;

In hope that sends a shining ray
Far down the future's broadening way;
    In peace that only thou canst give,
With thee, O Master, let me live.

                        Washington Gladden

2
FACING THE ASSAULT OF SIN

Hebrews 2:5–9

Temptation is characteristic of this world. Pervasive and unending, it comes to us in hosts of disguises. Most attacks have to do with things that go on in our minds: pride, envy, hatred, bitterness, and criticism. We are also tempted to speak hurtful words, or good words from wrong motives. All of us are tempted to violate our own moral standards.

The truth is, however, that most of us don't even realize that we are under attack most of the time. It is as natural as sunrise to put ourselves first. Ordinary people like you and me don't worry too much about most of the temptations to which we yield. It seems natural to act selfishly, to lose our tempers, to profit from others' mistakes or ignorance. We don't think much about it.

We don't think much about it, that is, until we begin to respond to God's invitation to walk in companionship with him and with his church. When we get serious about walking with Jesus Christ, temptation becomes a very painful matter indeed. It is one of the strange realities of this life of faith that the closer we want to walk with God, the greater our struggle with temptation. We ask in despair: "Can there be no real victory in this life?"

Our Hebrew writer began with creation—temptaion was not God's plan. Our first parents were made "a little lower than the angels," crowned "with glory and honor," and God put everything under their feet (2:7–8). In their freedom, autonomy, and power of dominion, they bore the mark of their Creator. These two humans were God's final creation, his highest creation. In them, in their minds, their spirits, their bodies, God had placed his own indelible stamp, his own image. We were made in the likeness of God himself.

We don't have the supernatural powers that angels seem to have. We are restricted to a material body so that we can be in only one place at a time, yet angels apparently are free to move by thought throughout the universe. Yet with all of their powers, their intelligence, and their mobility, angels lack one quality: the image of God. God has made us his highest creation and crowned our first parents with glory and honor, for they were the best that an eternal God could do.

FREEDOM MAKES US VULNERABLE

I suppose we shall debate forever the question of what exactly constitutes the image of God. Is it individual personality? Is it a capacity for judgment and choice? Or is it simply an independent will? However we approach it, the purpose and goal of the creation of man and woman was companionship with God. This man, this woman, joined in love, had the capacity, opportunity, and desire to walk with God. His plan from the beginning was that men and women might live in peace and victory every day of their lives. He provided for Adam and Eve everything they needed to live that kind of life.

But our first parents' capacity for companionship with God also gave them an alternative to obedience. The serpent said to Eve, "Has God said, 'Don't eat of that tree?' Well, God didn't really mean that. Actually, He is trying to keep something from you, and if you knew what that was, you could be more than you are." Doubt, disobedience, rebellion: the fruit of one suggestion. At this point, our God-given dominion ended. God had provided that everything should be under subjection to us, under our feet, that we should be in charge of our lives and in charge of our world, under his supreme authority.

The writer of Hebrews had to say, however, after he had described the creation of Adam, "Yet at present we do not see everything subject to him" (2:8). It was once true, but no more. The word that is used here carries the image of a soldier of ancient times in personal combat with an enemy. When the enemy was vanquished and as a final stroke of victory, the victor raised the sword over his head and placed his foot on the neck of his enemy. This was victory, this was triumph. The enemy lay on the ground, literally in subjection under foot. Perfect victory; complete victory.

But that is not true for us. Even when we recognize temptation for what it is, which is rare, and gain victory over it, which is rarer still, we are faced with the disconcerting fact that our enemies won't stay dead. It seems that we fight a battle with temptation, conquer it, and, lo, the same temptation walks in the back door. We fight the battle again and again. No, we do not see everything put under our feet.

Where is victory? Even to say that consistent victory is possible brings to the minds of too many people, and Christians among them, a fundamental and pervasive misunderstanding about this life of faith. I cannot even estimate the number of times people have said to me, "But I can't live the Christian life." It is an excuse, of course. But it also reveals what a lot of listeners hear when the preacher starts talking about obedience to God. Even when the opposite is intended, people hear, "If you would only try harder. . . ." "If you would only pay attention. . . ." "Just try it again. . . ." And every time a conscientious individual really gets serious about trying harder and being victorious, Satan sneaks in from somewhere and sets up an ambush. Another poor soul winds up flat on his face in the mud. And when it happens once too often, someone quits trying, quits believing, and drifts away in hopelessness.

Is victory merely trying harder or paying more attention or listening more closely? Is it marshaling all our energies to try to keep on top of temptation? Thousands of Christians have followed that path, not to speak of the millions of nonbelievers who think that is the way. Remember the bitter agony of a Martin Luther who had done everything he could, even to the point of destroying his physical and mental health, yet finding neither peace nor victory. And his testimony is echoed a million times in the history of the church.

The Hebrew church was in mortal danger of succumbing to this error. If God and his law could only be written in manageable proportions, then victory might be possible. It seemed, at least from a distance, that the Pharisees had accomplished that. And the appeal of the law, which Paul addressed so clearly, was in effect a way to corral temptation into narrow, recognizable, and manageable channels. This is legalism: seeking victory through human effort.

VICTORY THROUGH COMPANIONSHIP

As long as we fight that battle on our own, we will never have victory. Remember, the Scriptures say that we do not see everything in subjection under our feet. And so long as we fight the battle, it will never be so. We don't have the strength, the wisdom, the knowledge, or perhaps even the desire to live a victorious life.

That is the whole story as far as human effort is concerned. But Scripture does not stop there. "We do not see everything subject to us. BUT WE DO SEE JESUS." There is no way in God's great universe that I can put into words the endless facets of meaning wrapped up in those words. Has it ever dawned on Christians in your circle of influence that God Almighty has walked in their shoes?

Our Hebrew guide is not talking here about the redemptive work of Christ. That will come later. He is stressing the incarnation of God as a human being, Jesus. It is not figurative or theological language to say that Jesus comes to live within us and walks with us. Too often we make that seem vague and mystical. God Almighty has walked in our shoes, in your shoes. In the flesh. He has come face to face with the same kinds of people that we have to deal with. He has suffered at their hands more than we will ever suffer. God himself has walked on this planet.

It took me a long time to despiritualize this business of an understanding, incarnate God, and I still wrestle with it. My struggle has been most apparent in my practice of prayer. I heard a lot of teaching and preaching on prayer. I read the books. I used first this guide and then that one. I memorized ACTS: Adoration, Confession, Thanksgiving, Supplication. I learned several other formulas, too. I cringed when the preacher got up and told of this saint or that person of God who prayed for hours every day. But before prayer became anything but hard and frustrating self-discipline, I had to understand that God had already walked in my shoes.

Perhaps if we evangelicals spent a little more time wrestling with the meaning of the Incarnation, without neglecting the Cross, we would be better able to comprehend this almost incomprehensible idea of companionship with God. "But God doesn't understand what kind of jungle it is out there. It's dog eat dog. And if I don't play by their rules, I get stabbed in the back—if I don't stab first! Does God understand *that*?" Yes, he does! He was stabbed in the back several times.

"But God doesn't understand the ridicule that I face." Yes, he does. He caught a lot of it. "But God doesn't understand how it hurts to be misunderstood and how bad it hurts to be mistreated by someone close to me." Yes, he does— because it happened to him. He faced it himself. "But he doesn't understand what it means for me to have to do without what everyone else enjoys." Yes, he does. Was it not Jesus himself who did not even have a place to call his own and where he could lay his head? And who gave up family ties in order to serve God?

He understands all this and more, but his awareness is not only intellectual, not merely an aspect of his all-knowingness. The power of the Gospel is that he has walked in our shoes. He has been face-to-face with human society. He has felt it; it has touched him. And when God in Jesus Christ says, "I understand," it means that he has walked through it, too. The rejection, the betrayal, the hurt, the ridicule, the disappoint-

ments, the frustrations, and the unfulfilled desires he understands from personal experience.

*   *   *

That much is the Incarnation: he understands. Now comes
the Cross. For an understanding God without the ability to
make a difference in our defeatedness is no better than a God
who doesn't care.

Our Hebrew brother continues: "He is able to help those
who are being tempted" (2:18). The KJV says, "able to succour
those who are tempted." All religious systems admit the reality
of some kind of moral struggle. But there is no gospel in them.
And there would be no Gospel in Christianity if the story
stopped with an all-knowing God, even if he had gained his
knowledge through personal experience. The Gospel begins to
ring only when we realize that he is able to come to our aid. It is
in his aid that we have hope of victory.

It is one thing to say that God really understands life that
is filled with struggle and temptation. It is another thing to use
that truth as an excuse. Some say, "God understands what a
hard time I have; God understands how hard it is to be
Christian, and he understands the compromises that I make and
the little lies that I tell, and the petty things that I do that I know
are wrong but that make my life a little easier. God understands
how hard it is, and when I get to heaven, he is going to say to
me, 'Poor thing.'"

WRONG! Yes, God understands. But that is no excuse
for our failure and our sin. It doesn't matter how hard it is or
how much we may have to suffer to do right because God's
standard of judgment is, and always will be, holiness. No,
suffering and trial and temptation don't exempt us from the
righteous requirements of God. And when we get to heaven we
won't be able to plead, "But I had such a hard time."

YIELDING OUR WILLS TO VICTORY

What then? If Jesus is able (and most willing, the writer
would add) to aid those who are tempted, why doesn't he do

so? Why the repeated struggle with temptation, and the recurring defeats? If he is able and willing, why don't things change? God freely offers his grace—his enabling energy—to us, and it is overwhelmingly sufficient. But we have a choice.

He does not force his help upon us; he offers it. Then he waits for our response. In the moment of trial or under the pressure to compromise in the face of desire welling from our own humanity, we sense the choice that confronts us. That is grace. We need only to breathe three words: "Oh God, help!" That is responsiveness. And we have all the legions of heaven to back us up. The power is there for the asking: "God, help me!" It may be three short words, but they are the three most powerful words in all the languages on the face of the earth. He is able to aid those who are tempted.

Such reliance on the immediate power of God in Christ is far easier to talk about than to practice. I have found that painfully true in my own experience. I don't suggest or imply that a new Christian will think—or want—to call in God's aid at every temptation. Pride, self-will, and self-reliance must still be faced and surrendered. Even then, reliance comes only through companionship with Jesus day by day. It is a discipline to be learned, a response to be practiced. God will no more program our responses in this area than he will in any other aspect of our relationship with him.

I must digress again for an important point. Perfect victory over temptation will not be realized in this life. But by God's grace, our victory becomes more and more extensive. This is growth: the grace of maturity. In our companionship with God, we press on toward the mark, and marvel at the change and progress he brings to our lives. However, our prevailing popular theology suggests that the only essential element in a continuing relationship with God is a one-time conversion experience. Even among Wesleyans, who hold that growth in grace is to be expected, there is a strong tendency to reduce the grace/response confrontation to one or two (or three—among some pentecostal Wesleyans) religious experiences. Such an emphasis on experience misses the miracle of the constant flow of God's grace into our lives. And that is an unfortunate oversight.

Rather than try to outline steps to victory over temptation (we prefer neat formulas, don't we?), I want to point directly to the source of victory—a day-to-day friendship with Jesus. If that relationship is healthy and growing, then the outcome of the battle is certain. Perhaps a story will illustrate how companionship with God brings victory.

My family and I lived for several years near the NASA installation at Huntsville, Alabama. Nearby was the NASA Space and Rocket Center, a high-tech science museum. We liked to take visitors and friends there because we never tired of it ourselves. One of the key attractions was a domed theater in which giant-screen, panoramic movies were shown. I usually sat in the upper ranks of the seats so I would not have to crane my neck. The picture was all around: above my head, below my feet, beyond the limits of my peripheral vision.

I shall never forget one feature we watched there. It was entitled *The Fliers*. It was a story about old biplanes restored for aerial stunt work. It seemed that I was actually aboard the plane as it banked and maneuvered through a narrow valley, engines roaring. We rocked back and forth, with walls of rock seemingly inches beyond the wings. Then the end of the valley would come suddenly, and the pilot would set that plane on one wing in a steep bank, and I would find myself hanging on the arms of that theater chair for dear life, with white knuckles! And my stomach—well, I had to swallow it back into place! It was nothing but trick photography, and I knew it. But I still hung on!

The reason for my reaction—and it was the same the second and third times—was really very simple. Almost everyone reacted in a similar way. The picture filled our vision. We had no point of reference that was not part of the moving image before us. And our bodies followed our eyes.

Victory over temptation begins as Jesus fills our spiritual vision. This is a relationship beyond rules and formulas: we are invited by God himself to walk as his companions. How shall we respond?

Fill all my vision, Savior, I pray,
  Let me see only Jesus today;
When through the valley thou leadest me,
  Give me thy glory and beauty to see.

Fill all my vision, Savior divine,
  Till with thy glory my spirit shall shine;
Fill all my vision, that all may see
  Thy holy image reflected in me.

Fill all my vision—let naught of sin
  Shadow the brightness shining within;
Let me see only thy blessed face,
  Feasting my soul on thine infinite grace.

                          Avis B. Christiansen[1]

NOTE

3

NOT ASHAMED TO
CALL US BROTHERS

Hebrews 2:10–15

Some years ago a petite Korean woman walked into my office. Her eyes were blazing—quite out of character with her quiet and conservative bearing, I noted to myself. She sat down and began to tell me what a member of my church had done to her. Was she angry! She thought I ought to do something, such as scourge the bum in public and throw him out of the church! She thought that no one like this member should be allowed to call himself a Christian.

Don't pastors have an interesting job? Not long after that visit another person showed up on my doorstep. I had never met her before. Her first words were, "I have a problem." She started, "My neighbor attends your church, and she is one of the most difficult people on earth to live with. Her children raise Cain in the neighborhood, and they don't take care of their lawn the way they are supposed to." I said . . . Well, what are you *supposed* to say in a time like that?

Shortly thereafter I was talking to a businessman who didn't know me. In our discussion the name of one of my members came up. However, I didn't tell this man that the person in question was a member of my church. Something in his voice warned me to keep my mouth shut. He let me know in emphatic language that he would never do business with that man again.

In each of these cases, I knew enough of the background
to recognize that the problems were not so one-sided. All three
problem people were sincere but immature believers. Yet their
conduct or attitude had been less than Christlike.

THE NEED OF SANCTIFICATION

I hear, I watch, I listen, I observe my Christan flock. I
wish that I could see myself as I see them. And I think about our
lives as Christians, we who carry the name of Jesus Christ. A
sense of shame for bringing discredit to the cause of our Lord
rises as a depressing vapor over my spirit. These words from
the heart of this Hebrew pastor begin to take on profound
meaning: "Both the one who makes men holy ["sanctifies,"
KJV, NASB] and those who are made holy ["sanctified," KJV,
NASB] are of the same family. So Jesus is not ashamed to call
them brothers" (2:11).

"He is not ashamed to call them brothers." He is talking
about us, even when our conduct or words at home, in the
neighborhood, or in the business community bring shame on
him. That is an undeserved compliment, a profound truth, an
awesome statement of the love of God. He will take us in our
weakness, our failure, our selfishness, our moments of
meanness, and will still call us brothers.

This does not excuse such behavior nor is it grounds to
justify our failure and sin. There is a condition attached to that
phrase; it doesn't stand alone. So let's look at the previous
statement. "Both he that sanctifies, and those who are sanctified
are of the same family. So Jesus is not ashamed to call them
brothers." Before we tackle that word *sanctify*, let's look first at
the context. What is God doing in this world?

"In bringing many sons [and daughters] to glory, it was
fitting that God [the Father] for whom and through whom
everything exists, should make the author [God the Son] of
their salvation perfect through suffering." God has a plan that
will prepare all of his children for a great, glorious homecoming
out there in the future. All that he does for us here is designed to
culminate in bringing together a holy family on the other side.

When we accept Jesus Christ as our Lord and Savior and invite him to come into our lives, this world ceases to be our home. We don't belong here; we don't fit here; and I trust to God that we are not comfortable here. We have been called to a new home, a home not made with hands, eternal in the heavens. A day is coming when all the brothers and sisters of Jesus Christ, you and I and God's whole redeemed church, will gather around that great heavenly throne where we will share the grandest, most gloriously spectacular extravaganza that will ever happen.

That is the homecoming—that is our destination. God's only plan in operation in this world is to bring sons and daughters to glory, to redeem and purify his church, to make us representative of his character. And when we join that eternal celebration, we will find that all of God's children are whole: spiritually, mentally, physically, and emotionally restored.

We are sons and daughters of God, brothers and sisters of Jesus. This concept that Jesus is bringing us together to heaven as a family is rooted in the relationship between the grace of God and our responsiveness. God is not going to take people to heaven against their wills. If God calls us, if he is bringing us together, if he is preparing us for that great homecoming, we must pay close attention to how we follow the Lord Jesus Christ.

THE PROCESS IN SANCTIFICATION

What do we mean when we say that we are following Jesus Christ? With that question we have moved into the vicinity of the word *sanctify*, which we laid aside a moment ago. "Both the one who sanctifies and those who are sanctified are of the same family." That means that if God sent Jesus Christ his Son into the world to redeem the world, he sent Jesus to you and me to transform our lives.

Both times the writer used *sanctify* here, he employed present tense verbs. It would be appropriate to translate the sentence, "Both the one who is sanctifying, and those who are being sanctified are of the same family." That present tense says

more about our Christian experience than I can possibly
explain. The only time that we can follow Jesus is *now*. We
cannot follow him yesterday, and we cannot follow him
tomorrow, no more than we can change yesterday's choices or
make tomorrow's decisions. We can follow him only today.

The whole of Christianity rests on the fact that a
relationship with God is something that is in the *now*. And it
will always be in the now. NOW is the day of salvation, NOW
is the time of God's favor (2 Cor. 6:2). Whatever has been in
the past, and whatever lies in the future, we are responsible for
our response to God's grace only in the NOW. That will be
true as long as we walk on the face of the earth. It is a present-
tense walk with God.

Our distinctions of "past," "present," and "future" are
irrelevant to an eternal God, and they will become irrelevant to
us the moment we set foot in heaven. Time has no meaning in
eternity. "When we've been there ten thousand years" has a
great deal of meaning to us, but it will be meaningless then, for
we shall have begun to live in an everlasting present. It is from
the perspective of an eternal heaven that the author of this letter
is writing.

Bauer says that *sanctify* means "1. of things: set them aside
or make them suitable for ritual purposes; 2. of persons:
consecrate, dedicate, sanctify, i.e., include in the inner circle of
what is holy, in both the religious and moral uses of the word;
3. treat as holy; 4. purify."[1]

That sounds as if God simply wants us to share his
character!

When we stand before God as convicted sinners, we ask
God to forgive our sins and come in and fill our lives with
himself. At that point we break with the old life. Some things,
many things change: activities, attitudes, ambitions, desires.
The new birth is the grace of God at work, making us new
creations. By grace we lose our appetite for things we know to
be sinful. We are really and truly changed, and every change
that the Holy Spirit effects in us in conversion makes us more
like God. And that is sanctification. It is far, far from complete,
but in conversion God is sanctifying us.

Conversion is the beginning, not the culmination, of the sanctifying work of God. There remains ahead for the young Christian a major struggle distinct from the lifelong attack of temptation. It is the battle with self-will. Before God can use you or me, or any other Christian, he must lead us to a place of confrontation with ourselves. Here we face the issue of sovereignty: Is Jesus Lord of our lives, or is he a guest? It is the grace of God that leads us to this confrontation, the response he seeks in our total surrender to his authority.

In that surrender he is again sanctifying us; for our abilities, our ambitions, our resources are now dedicated solely for his use, or disuse, as he wills and as we understand his will. Our inner being is no longer torn between conflicting loyalties to ourselves and to God. We can pray, "Father, I don't want my own way or seek my own glory. I want to do your will more than I want anything else in this world—more than wealth or prestige or comfort, I want you!"

Those in the Wesleyan tradition have no monopoly on such an understanding of sanctification. Christians in every tradition have faced that confrontation with themselves. But Wesleyans have made both too much and too little of a doctrine of a second special work of God's grace subsequent to conversion. We have made *too much* of it because many have wrapped up all the sanctifying work of God and forced it into this one experience.

At the same time, we have made too little of it because we have interpreted the sanctifying work of God as only an inward, mystical, subjective (and, yes, emotional) work. The greatest contradictions I know in the Christian world are congregations of Christians professing heart purity without any evidence of spiritual power in their public witness. When God really has control of our resources, we won't use them the way many American congregations spend their money and time.

In leading us to settle the issue of sovereignty, God is sanctifying us. In heaven his will only shall be done, and he is preparing us now to fit into heaven. But that is still only the beginning, not the culmination, of God's sanctifying work.

God's work now moves to the arena of temptation and

testing. That which is designed by Satan for our destruction is commandeered by the Holy Spirit for our benefit. In each moment of temptation, God's grace comes to us, offering an alternative to disobedience. Each time we breathe those three short words, "God, help me," something more of this world falls away from us, and more of the other world shines through.

This is the life of sanctification. Wesleyans call it growth in grace; Calvinists may call it progressive sanctification. God is sanctifying us and making us fit for heaven. Our sanctification does not end until God's grace fails us, which is never so long as we have responsive hearts. His purpose is to make us fit for that homecoming. He wants us to be happy there, and we learn the lessons of heaven while we are on the way. The life of sanctification is the life of companionship with God.

What is this responsive heart? It is a work of God's grace, yet it is at the same time a free and undetermined choice that each of us makes. That choice is to obey. Obedience for too many has been tainted by legalism, and I suppose it will always be so. But any legalistic faith places obedience first, but God always places obedience second. When obedience is first, we are seeking to earn a reward by doing what is demanded of us. When obedience is second, we are responding to the love of God revealed to us, and are loving him in return. We are being sanctified in our responsive obedience to God.

THE RESULTS OF SANCTIFICATION

It is rare to find fear discussed in relation to God's sanctifying work. Our Hebrew writer puts it together: ". . . by [Jesus'] death he . . . free[s] those who all their lives were held in slavery by their fear of death" (2:15). By taking the greatest fear that we humans bear, our brother brings all fear out into the open.

A young woman's radiant face is indelibly imprinted on my mind. Larry and Chris were a young couple who stood out to me because of their open-hearted desire to learn all they could about being truly Christian. They had three children, and had purchased a lovely home a short distance out in the country.

Larry worked the evening shift, and it was often into the wee hours of the morning when he arrived home. I knew nothing of the struggle that Chris was facing during those lonely nights until she stood in church with her face beaming, and told of the victory that God had given her over a life-long fear of darkness.

I have to ask myself why that particular testimony made such an impact on me. Was it because such victories are so rare? Was it because others were nursing their fears, using enormous amounts of nervous energy to avoid facing those fears? And how rare, too, is an understanding that walking in companionship with God is a walk of ever-increasing freedom from fear—fear of all kinds.

C. S. Lewis wove a remarkable understanding of fear in his science fiction work entitled *Out of the Silent Planet*.[2] Dr. Ransom, an eccentric linguistics professor at Cambridge, was kidnapped by a mad scientist and taken to Mars, apparently as a specimen to appease the curiosity of terrible monsters there. Ransom escaped his kidnappers, but was, of course, trapped in an alien world.

Dr. Ransom's every action and thought were colored—and usually consumed—by fear of this unknown world and its inhabitants. But only after months of running and hiding in terror did it finally begin to dawn on him that these were harmless, innocent, and unpresuming beings. The walls of fear began to crumble, and he discovered to his amazement that evil did not exist in this alien world. There was nothing to fear. Here even the unknown was no cause for fear, and death brought a measure of sorrow but no fear. Everyone knew—and acted as if he knew—that a loving, just God was in control.

Our sanctifying God, then, not only works to strip from us the barnacles of sin, but also strives to open our hearts and minds to the wonders of a world under his control. Yet how slow we are to learn! How we resist those terrifying lessons! And nowhere is that more evident than in our avoidance of death. This is Satan's ultimate weapon, his ultimate source of control over us.

The wrenching sting of death is the appearance, as far as we can see with earthly vision, that death ends all. All that we build and all that we secure and all that we gain for ourselves suddenly comes to an end, and we are left with nothing. The world without Christ is a frustrating place to live because, despite all our power and all that we can accomplish, each of us comes to the same place: the grave. What power over people that gives Satan! We refuse to deal with the fact that we are going to die. We spend billions of dollars to try to make ourselves look younger. And most of it is wasted!

The gospel, then, is good news for us, really good news. The final enemy that stands between us and that great homecoming over there has been conquered by the Lord Jesus Christ. He has taken its power; he has won the victory. He has transformed what appears to be the end into a glorious new beginning of real life. If Jesus can take death, its terror, its darkness, its power—if he can turn death inside out and make it a gateway into real life, there is no circumstance or problem on earth that he cannot transform.

The sanctifying work of Christ can deal with fear and death and every other burden that causes us grief, pain, and disappointment. We are in no way exempted from these heart-wrenching valleys, but if with responsive hearts we allow God to change us, we find that he turns all of the ends into new beginnings. We can walk through the valleys, the trials, the illnesses, the losses, the betrayals; and we then experience growing victory. We are being sanctified, for Jesus is sanctifying us and preparing us to be at home in heaven.

In recent months, I have heard several older people say, "Possessions are not so important to me as they used to be. More and more I am realizing that God is really all I need." Wouldn't it be great if we could learn that at twenty instead of seventy? But these have been men and women who have walked closely with God for years, and God has been doing his sanctifying work year by year.

But there is another choice that we can make, for I talk with other professing Christians who are bitter, resentful, angry, possessive, and fearful. They have backed away and refused to allow God to do His work in their lives. These may go through the motions, play church, and fabricate elaborate pretenses, but they are not letting God do his work in their lives. They profess assurance of heaven, but they are ill-fitted to be happy there—or here.

We end this study with a testimony of ringing, joyful submissiveness. Can you make these words your own?

> My God and Father, while I stray
> Far from my home, in life's rough way,
> O teach me from my heart to say,
> "Thy will be done."
>
> If but my fainting heart be blest
> With Thy sweet Spirit for its guest,
> My God, to thee I leave the rest,
> "Thy will be done."
>
> Renew my will from day to day;
> Blend it with thine, and take away
> All now that makes it hard to say,
> "Thy will be done."
>
> Then when on earth I breathe no more
> The prayer oft mixed with tears before,
> I'll sing upon a happier shore,
> "Thy will be done."
>
> Charlotte Elliot

NOTES

[1] Walter Bauer, *A Greek-English Lexicon of the New Testament and Other Early Christian Literature* (Chicago: University of Chicago Press, 1957), 8. This is not a complete quote, but includes all main points.

[2] C. S. Lewis, *Space Trilogy* (New York: Macmillan, 1975).

4

THE EASY PATH TO A HARDENED HEART

Hebrews 3:1–19

I was looking for part-time work to help me through college, and Frederick Richardson needed assistance in his small business. He hired me on the spot, and I spent the first few days trying to size him up. A shapeless cardigan and open-necked shirt seemed to emphasize his much-too-ample girth. He was rarely without a cigarette in one hand and a can of beer in the other. When he wasn't talking with a customer, he plopped into an old rocking chair in the corner, occupying himself with the most recent dirty novel from the drug store. My first reaction proved true: Fred was a hard, sensual man.

Imagine my consternation when I learned that he had been the senior pastor of a large church in the area. He had been a writer with enough credits to his name to impress a green college student. Fred, it turned out, had been an outspoken evangelical with impressive pastoral abilities. He had wielded a lot of influence in his denomination. One day I found an old box of tapes marked "Sermons." With his permission I listened to one of them. This man had also been a powerful preacher. My fascination merged into puzzlement: what on earth had changed him?

Since I was a young theology student, I took Fred as my evangelism project. We talked as often as I could corner him, but I never sensed any remorse or sorrow or even nostalgia. I prayed for him as best I knew how. But I came to realize the awful truth: I was battering a stone wall. Fred was a very hard man.

Our Hebrew author must have also have had some friends like Fred, for he describes in chapter 3 the process of hardening. He refers to the rebellion of the children of Israel as they neared the Promised Land. He warned, "See to it, brothers, that none of you has a *sinful heart of unbelief*" (3:12, emphasis mine). These phrases are keys to understanding how hearts are hardened.

UNBELIEF IS A CHOICE WE MAKE

Our author quoted several verses from Psalm 95, in which the psalmist refers to the Exodus. The story of the Exodus was engrained in the consciousness of every Jew, and the rebelliousness of the people was a much-rehearsed lesson. The euphoria of deliverance quickly gave way to complaints about the water, the lack of bread and meat, the threat of enemies, the heat, the food God provided, and, of course, Moses himself.

The context for all this dissatisfaction was the most astounding demonstration of the power and love of God that any generation ever witnessed until the birth of Christ. Plague after plague challenged the gods of Egypt one by one. The Egyptian army died in the sea, and the Hebrews didn't raise a sword or loose an arrow. God gave water from the rock, bread from the dew, supernatural victory over seasoned enemy forces. And there was the cloud: an immediate, daily and nightly reminder that God had intervened.

Down beneath the complaining and the rebellion was the simple fact that these people refused to believe that God would do what he said he would do. They *refused*! Unbelief is not an intellectual problem: it is a choice to reject the hand of fellowship that God extends to us.

God is at work in this devilish world reconciling a people unto himself. We call this divine initiative *grace*. God extends life, love, and community to all men and women. He has provided a plan for redemption and reconciliation, and then woos and confronts us with the possibilities of companionship and consequences of refusal. All this, and more, is *grace*.

Grace comes to us through the natural world, the medium of human conscience, and parents who may even be rebels themselves. Grace comes through hopes and dreams, books and conversations, spouses and children. But finally, and perfectly, grace comes to us in Jesus Christ.

At some point down deep in the center of our human personality, the grace of God meets our will. An all-powerful God confronts an independent will—his own creation. Impossible? No. Certainly God is able to impose his will on us. He is able and free to do as he pleases. The question is whether God can choose *not* to impose his will. The very fact that we are responsible for our conduct before God as Judge is the best proof we can present that a just God chooses not to override, ignore, or manipulate the wills of human beings.

Therefore, within the context of God's self-imposed restraint, we make eternal choices. The responsive individual enters a world of companionship with a loving Father. The rebel turns and walks into darkness, climbing over barrier after barrier placed in his path by the God he spurns. We will never know what distance God goes to prevent us from destroying ourselves. We do have, however, this guarantee: He will never impose his will on us by force. That is the nature of true love.

Unbelief, then, is a posture men and women assume toward God's authority. Unbelief is not the absence of faith; it is antifaith. The antibeliever suffers from a sort of self-imposed personality disorder. He or she reduces all reality to a manageable size. The antibeliever retires into a world of his own making, unable to comprehend that his creation is ever shrinking toward oblivion. Disastrously, the antibeliever immerses himself in the one spiritual solvent guaranteed to free his character of trust. Since all sound relationships are based on trust, unbelief undermines his very humanity. This is the path to a hardened heart.

HARDENING IS A DECEPTION WE SWALLOW

The second key statement is "hardened by sin's deceitfulness." The hardening of unbelief does not begin with sins of the flesh. All of God's grace does not come to us in a single cosmic confrontation. So we cannot spurn his grace in a single choice. Rather, we rebel in small, insignificant steps. With each tiny step, we grow harder.

I toy with building furniture in my spare time (but wait until I retire!). I love the luster and satin of carefully finished wood: mahogany, oak, cherry, pine. Each board has a personality of its own, with unique grain and subtle contrasts of color and shade.

I also have on my desk a polished chunk of petrified wood that I use as a paperweight. It is hard, incredibly dense. It did not become so in a single moment. But grain by grain, minerals leeched from the surrounding soil replaced rotting fibers of once-living wood. The process was gradual and silent, yet persistent.

I often ponder the irregular contours of that wood–now-stone, wondering at the complete and terrible transformation that has occurred. Could it happen to me as it happened to Fred? I use it as the basis for an occasional children's sermon. Could it be that some of these little ones will fall victim to that same horrible transformation? O God, what an awful possibility!

Andrew Murray provides a sobering reflection for us:

> When we are secretly content with our religion, our sound doctrine and Christian life, unconsciously but surely the heart gets hardened. When our life does not seek to keep pace with our knowledge, and we have more pleasure in hearing and knowing than obeying and doing, we utterly lose the meekness to which the promise is given, and, amidst all the pleasing forms of godliness, the heart is too hard to discern the voice of the Spirit . . . Yes, it is an unspeakably solemn thought, that with a mind occupied with religious truth, and feelings stirred at times by the voice and works, the heart may be closed to the humble, direct

intercourse with God, and a stranger to all the blessing the living word can bring.[1]

Murray was writing to the same kind of people that our Hebrew brother was addressing. I purposely skipped the first verses of the chapter. Now let's go back and pick up a telling phrase by our Hebrew friend.

". . . holy brothers, who share in the heavenly calling" (3:1). This warning about hardness and deceitfulness is not directed to the unbeliever. It is a warning to the holy brothers, that body of men and women who have responded to the initiatives of grace. The warning is directed to us. See to it (the NASB reads, "Take care!") that none of you has a sinful, unbelieving heart that turns away from the living God!

Friend, this is solemn. It is awe-full! Hardness does not begin with outward sin. It does not begin when we cast off the moral restraints that should guide the Christian life. Hardness begins within. In the midst of our religion, our church attendance, our service to God, we begin to harden. Christian, we are in danger.

Mark and Allison were an attractive couple in their mid-twenties. Both grew up in families that were active in conservative churches in my community. Mark was singing in a Christian musical group, and both claimed a new-birth experience. The story they told, however, disturbed me. They wanted to get married, but since both of them had been married before, their pastors would not be involved. And they had been living together for more than a year. Would I be willing . . .

I challenged them as gently yet as pointedly as I could. Did they see no contradiction between their profession and their lifestyle? I led them into the Scriptures, hoping that they could understand why God had placed strict boundaries around our sexuality in order to protect us from ourselves. I tried the positive approach: wouldn't it be worth the inconvenience of different living arrangements to set things right with God now, and then come to the marriage altar knowing that the past is forgiven?

But as we talked, I sensed something of that same stone

wall I encountered with Fred. At the conclusion of our conversation, Allison remarked, "Well, pastor, I appreciate your honesty in sharing your opinion with us, but I guess we look at our circumstances from a different point of view." I cringed inside. My *opinion*? When God made his will absolutely clear in black and white? O God, what have we taught our children?

Could it be that these young people learned their unbelief from "Bible-believing" pastors and teachers and parents? Are they not living out in the sexual realm the casual attitude toward the claims of Christ they unconsciously learned from us? Have we taken God's Word seriously in the economic and social spheres of life? How can we judge them, caught up as we are in our soft, selfish, self-indulgent evangelicalism?

Our evangelical churches are filled with young families head over pocketbooks in debt, keeping up with their friends. Christian fathers, leaders in our churches, are sacrificing principle and family to climb the corporate ladder. Christian mothers put career ahead of the nurture of their children. How casually we lay aside those principles of Scripture that disturb our middle-class comfort.

I realize in retrospect something disturbing about becoming hardened. At the very time I was most concerned about my friend Fred and his hardness, I was already becoming hard myself. I had started down the same path that he had followed for so long, the path that Mark and Allison had also chosen. I put intellectual pursuits ahead of personal discipleship. I was allowing words to take the place of action. I was using my testimony to hide the shallowness of my obedience. Even though I was preparing for the ministry, I was becoming hardened. As Dwight Moody is credited with saying of a drunkard staggering down the street, "There, but for the grace of God, go I."

How many of us are going through the motions of religious life? We are faithful and dependable. We compare ourselves with ourselves and find we are a little above average. But our hearts are not listening for the quiet voice of God. If unbelief is so deceitful that it can trap us in the midst of our

Christianity, what chance do we have? What hope do we have? If we had the technology to make printed words glow, I would want the next two sentences to flash like a neon sign. WE HAVE EVERY REASON TO HOPE! WE HAVE JESUS!

IN JESUS WE AVOID THE INEVITABLE

Again: "Therefore, holy brothers, who share in the heavenly calling, fix your thoughts on Jesus." Look at him. Take your eyes off the duties and obligations of being a Christian. Take your mind off the things that you want or don't want. Look long at Jesus; study him; analyze him.

Jesus bears two special titles in this passage. First, he is the apostle of our faith. This is the only place in the New Testament where this title is used of him, but it is certainly appropriate. He came as a messenger. He brought to us, in flesh and blood, a revelation of the character of God. He has explained what God expects of us and what God wants to do for us. We can no longer claim ignorance. But he is more than the apostle: he is also our High Priest.

The priest's responsibility was not so much to tell people about God as it was to tell God about the people. In fact, the priest was commissioned to represent his fellow worshipers in the presence of God. The priesthood is something essentially different from the work of the prophet or the apostle. The priest was always a member of the group that he represented before God. He was a friend, a companion, a relative. He lived in the community, reared his family, joined in the festivals and the sorrows of life. Yet at the call of God he brought his companions into God's presence.

Our Hebrew brother reveled in the priesthood of Jesus. Without the limitations that plague human priests, Jesus uses his personal experience of our condition to intercede for us before the throne of mercy. We are trapped in the deceitfulness of sin, but our Priest is drawing us to God. He is pulling at us; he is stirring us; he is constantly trying to get through to our thick heads and hard hearts. The cry rings out in the presence of God, "Father, these my brothers and sisters need help!"

The second statement in this passage begins, "He was faithful to the one who appointed him." Bowing there in the Garden of Gethsemane, praying with and for his disciples, he said: "Father, I have finished the work that you sent me into the world to accomplish." He had been faithful. He had lived a perfect life. He had revealed God as best the human mind could understand him.

But there is more. "But Christ is faithful as a son over God's house. And we are his house, if we hold onto our courage and the hope of which we boast." He is the infinite Priest who represents us by name, and brings us by name before the throne of the universe, moment by moment. He is constantly at work within us to draw each of us to himself. Paul was making this point in Galatians 5:17 when he mentioned that the Spirit desires (the KJV reads, "lusts for") what is contrary to the sinful flesh. Can you see the holy fire of jealousy in a loving, almighty God? He seeks to draw us to himself and to defeat the deceitful powers of sin that would harden us.

We do not, then, have to live in anxious fear that our hearts will become hard. God is constantly at work within us. But we must be careful to understand that we have to continue to respond to God's grace. On one hand we can settle down to a satisfied, comfortable, and complacent religious experience: pray the standard prayers, listen to the preacher, and do the job that we have been elected to do in the church. But that choice leads to hearts that can be as hard as my paperweight.

On the other hand, we can place ourselves humbly in God's hands. I'm not talking about rehashing an experience from childhood, or even two or three years ago. I'm talking about today. We stop right where we are, in the midst of all our activities, and say, "O God, I'm listening. What do you want to change today?" The warning is timely: "Today, if you will hear his voice, do not harden your heart."

By the way, I received a telephone call from Allison a few days later. Her voice was vibrant. She and Mark had been thinking about our discussion. They had prayed together, and in confession made a covenant with God and each other to live separately until their wedding. The battle is not lost!

O the deep, deep love of Jesus—
Vast, unmeasured, boundless, free!
Rolling as a mighty ocean
In its fullness over me,
Underneath me, all around me,
Is the current of thy love—
Leading onward, leading homeward,
To my glorious rest above.

O the deep, deep love of Jesus—
Spread his praise from shore to shore!
How he loveth, ever loveth,
Changeth never, nevermore.
How he watches o'er his loved ones,
Died to call them all his own;
How for them he intercedeth;
Watcheth o'er them from the throne.

O the deep, deep love of Jesus—
Love of every love the best!
'Tis an ocean vast of blessing,
'Tis a haven sweet of rest.
O the deep, deep love of Jesus—
'Tis a heaven of heavens to me;
And it lifts me up to glory,
For it lifts me up to thee.

                                    S. Trevor Francis

NOTE

[1] Andrew Murray, *The Holiest of All* (Westwood, NJ: Revell, 1960), 117.

5

THE ELUSIVE REST

Hebrews 4:1–11

I have always felt like an outsider when I read the fourth chapter of Hebrews. Haven't you been in a group of people where everyone knew the private, inside stories about each other? Everyone, that is, except you! It left you wondering what was going on. When I wrestle with the word *rest* in chapter 4, I struggle with a persistent suspicion that these Hebrews understood something that I know nothing about.

SABBATH REST AS· AN ILLUSTRATION

The secret of all good communication revolves around the art of illustration. We need look no further than the words of Jesus to see the master communicator using story after story. Our Hebrew author understood the importance of illustrations. He wanted a vague and distant truth to be reflected in the colors of the familiar. The vague and distant truth was the peace of God that surpasses all understanding. The illustration he chose to help his readers touch the inexpressible was the Sabbath rest.

You and I as twentieth-century evangelicals have a terrible problem at this point. But before I explore it, I need to clarify as best I can the outline of the illustration. The writer actually takes four different kinds of rest and lays them on top of one another, without making sharp distinctions: creation rest, Canaan rest, Sabbath rest, and spiritual rest.

Creation rest: God rested on the seventh day. It was a rest not of weariness but of perfection, completeness. In fact, God is the only one who has ever or will ever complete a job properly. God's creation rest was the model and foundation for the Sabbath, but it was something from the remote and distant past. It would not serve as that gripping, eye-opening illustration of God's peace.

Canaan rest: Joshua gave the people rest after the successful conquest of the Promised Land. This rest was never complete. It lasted for only one short generation. The people returned to their grandfathers' pattern of rebelliousness and suffered under the judgment of God. Our author could have aroused a lot of nationalistic emotion at this point, but honest Jews knew that the spiritual promise was yet to be fulfilled. No, Canaan rest cannot illustrate God's peace; it was only a shadow.

Sabbath rest: The keeping of the Sabbath was a central pillar of the Jews' own identity and a clear barometer of their relationship with God. With rules piled on rules the Pharisees had almost completely obscured the deeper meaning of the Sabbath. But by harping on it year after year, they had permanently engraved Sabbath-keeping on the Jewish heart. For our Hebrew writer, this was the handle that would allow his readers to grasp the incomprehensible peace that was to be the gift of God. The Sabbath was immediate and real for the Hebrews. The Sabbath represented the unfulfilled promises of the past. It embodied all the embryonic hopes for a glorious restored kingdom of peace in the reign of the Messiah.

Spiritual rest: The peace of God is a profound inner rest. In the inner recesses of our humanity, God designed a place for himself. When he is absent, nothing else can ever be exactly right. When he is present, well, how can I describe the indescribable? Our Hebrew brother tried by illustrating it with the Sabbath rest. But we have no conception of Sabbath rest. How much we have lost in losing the Sabbath! Could it be . . . do you suppose . . . what if Sabbath rest is more than an illustration? Could it also be a doorway? Might it be that I cannot know God's spiritual rest until I understand his Sabbath rest?

Now, lest you think I am completely off base, let me assure you that I understand Sabbath observance. You bet I do! I grew up in the parsonage, and I learned early how to act on Sunday. First, go to Sunday school and morning worship. Then eat a large family dinner. Enjoy a quiet afternoon. That meant no ball games, no running and climbing and rowdiness indoors or out. Read. Talk. Play quietly. Sleep (if you are an adult, that is). Go back to church. Don't do any shopping or any chores around the house. And, especially, don't go to work.

I am not ridiculing any of those rules because every one of them was intended, in the beginning at least, to protect one day each week from becoming like all the others. That early discipline paid rich dividends for me. One of the rules in my home was "No homework on Sunday." I'm sure I was galled at times by having to do homework on Saturday, but I don't remember those feelings. I do remember the heavy course loads and part-time jobs and family responsibilities of college and graduate school years. This principle from childhood was so deeply ingrained that I was still able to take Sunday off without feeling that I was neglecting my studies.

But even that has changed now that I am a pastor. Pastors don't keep Sabbaths. (I fear that pastors most value the members of their churches who don't keep Sabbaths either. Too much resting on Sunday means that church programs are understaffed, doesn't it?) I knew that I was supposed to take a day off. My church boards have sometimes insisted that I take one. But I never had time. And besides, what does taking a day off have to do with keeping the Sabbath? I really never related the two! After all, I still maintained many of the Sunday disciplines I learned in childhood. So I was keeping the Sabbath. Right? Wrong! Sunday is a day of emotional and spiritual drain. (Some of my people still think it is the only day I work.) I wondered . . . could it be . . . that here lies the root of my inner unease, my haunting sense of dissonance with myself?

The heartbeat of life is a rhythm of throbbing confrontations between the grace of God and the will of the individual.

The Christian makes the choice to respond to God's initiative. We cooperate with Him in what He is doing. We fall into line. Several years ago an article by Eugene Peterson began to help me understand the importance of my response to the grace of God, in the context of the Sabbath. Peterson wrote:

> Instead of grace/work we make it work/grace. Instead of working in a world in which God calls everything into being with his word and redeems his people with an outstretched arm, we rearrange it as a world in which we preach the mighty work of God and in afterthought ask him to bless our speaking; a world in which we stretch out our mighty arms to help the oppressed and open our hands to assist the needy and desperately petition God to take care of those we miss.[1]

In our Western culture we have placed great value on productivity and results. We chart growth in numbers and dollars. Bigger is better, more glorious; time is money; visible prosperity is *de facto* evidence of the blessing of God. We encourage burdened people to work harder and failing people to try again. We have formulas for answered prayer, financial success, salvation of the world, well-adjusted children, and overcoming depression. But where is rest?

I just learned of a pastoral colleague in a neighboring county who is ill. He is about my age (that means he is still young), but his health is breaking. The doctors have laid down the law: three months' complete rest away from church responsibilities.

What goes for pastors also goes for parishioners. The number one problem that our congregations face is burnout among active members. I grieve over faithful, dedicated layfolk who gradually become disenchanted and discouraged in their service for God. Once they break under the load, it is hard, so hard, to lead them again to the joy of loving service to God. We understand God's service but not his rest.

SABBATH REST IS A DOORWAY

God loves celebrations. When he gave to Moses the religious and social laws for his people, he filled the calendar with festivals! The major harvest festivals, the monthly new moon festivals, the weekly Sabbath celebrations. If you look closely at Leviticus 23, you will find that within the first twenty-two days of the seventh month God scheduled six Sabbaths! These were not somber affairs when God's people wore long faces with weepy eyes. Camping out in the front yard, feasting for a week at a time, family meals that told a story, elaborate and expressive ceremonies at the tent of meeting or the temple—these were happy times.

It is true that Christ was the final fulfillment of the types and shadows embodied in many of those ceremonies. But what passed away was replaced by other joyful occasions. Sunday was set apart as a day of rejoicing in the presence of a now-living Savior. The agape and the Lord's Supper were perhaps daily, not weekly or monthly, reminders that Christians have cause for celebration. The daily services disappeared, but in the early church, feast days multiplied as Christians celebrated the godly leaders who had gained the victor's wreath. And wherever sparks of true Christianity have been ignited by the Holy Spirit, celebration has been the order of the day.

The biblical festivals were not suggested but commanded by God himself. That should provide us with cause to stop and ponder their meaning. We are immersed in a tangible world of sense and feeling. It is also a secular world and always has been. It is separate and distinct from God. It is, therefore, only a shadow of reality. God knew that we would need all the help we could find to keep ourselves from being drowned in this material universe. This was the rationale for the celebration.

Every festival had a distinct purpose. Some reminded the people of what God had done in the past. Others were harvest celebrations of thanksgiving. Still others pointed to the future, when God would complete the work of redemption and restoration. The festivals and Sabbaths were anchors that moored the people to the spiritual realities they could not see. Each was a declaration that the meaning of life could never be found in this world itself. We must look up to understand.

But look what we have allowed to happen to us! Our festivals are almost all totally secularized. Thanksgiving is being buried under Christmas shopping. Christmas has been preempted by a jolly fellow in a red suit who has something to do with statistics on consumer spending. Easter remains but it is slipping. What on earth does a rabbit have to do with eggs, and what do either have to do with resurrection? Many camp meetings that still survive have the appearance of geriatric conventions. Some churches still have periodic revival campaigns, but many are drab affairs.

And there's the Sabbath. Once they have allowed time to attend church services, how many evangelicals believe that the rest of the day is merely God's gift to give them time to do the laundry and mow the lawn? We have allowed this secular culture to strip us of our festivals, our celebrations, our Sabbaths. And with each loss, we find that God recedes further and further into the distance. Where is our rest?

Don't misunderstand me. I am not for multiplying rules. Nor do I recommend a showy nonconformity just to make us "different" from our neighbors. The Pharisees were masters at those endeavors, but never recognized the Lord of the Sabbath looking at them eyeball to eyeball. For the last two generations, Victorian Sundays have received their share of bad press. But the problem was not so much the rules as the fact that Sundays became hollow cultural shells of respectability. They were not celebrations. I have no formula nor program to suggest. But I know we must find rest, or we shall surely fall to pieces.

To paraphrase Eugene Peterson, keeping the Sabbath is deliberately to schedule nonproductive time into our calendars. What? Waste time? Horrors! But we must set things in their proper order. After all, our time is nonproductive apart from the presence of our creating God. Peterson writes, "Sabbath: uncluttered time and space to distance ourselves from the frenzy of our own activities so we can see what God has been doing and is doing."[2]

It is sobering and humbling to acknowledge that in the eternal frame of reference all our efforts are of dubious value. It is equally humbling to acknowledge that all that is of lasting value is accomplished by the energy of God. For the rebellious, these facts would destroy all initiative and all meaning. But for the responsive Christian, it is glorious. As we fall in with the flow of the divine purpose and the divine work, our efforts are energized by the divine. "I no longer live, but Christ lives in me. The life I live in the body, I live by faith in the Son of God, who loved me, and gave himself for me," wrote St. Paul (Gal. 2:20). My efforts now have eternal significance, for I am in partnership with an Eternal God.

The Sabbath, then, is a visible, tangible, real-life declaration of faith in the companionship of our Eternal Father. We declare, not by our words but by our actions (or inaction) that he is involved in our world—in my world. But do we not more often say, "Yes, God is involved in my life, but he is not interested in my shop or my classroom or my office or my ball game or my vacation or my . . . ? But God is involved in every facet of our lives! His energy accomplishes through our yielded lives what we cannot achieve ourselves. How else can we declare our faith in this sovereign, involved God except by regularly stopping our activity?

I must confess that my preaching is still vastly more biblical than my practice. But I have begun to understand—and to experience in a measure—the meaning of the rest of faith. It is God's sovereign power that completes our eternal salvation. We are not saved by our efforts nor our sacrifices nor our obediences nor our spiritual disciplines. It is he and he alone who is at work within each of us, both to create the desire and to give us the power to do his will. But the rest of faith is much more than this alone.

If God is involved in every facet of our lives, then it is his presence that lends permanent value to our work. We can rest in his ability and not our own. In business, in ministry, in family life, in sports and hobbies our ability cannot initiate anything of eternal worth, but God can and does. It is his grace that confronts us again and again. If we choose submission, we find rest. As we continue to submit, the rest increases and broadens. God does his work within us, through us, beyond us, and even in spite of us.

The path that I have trod
Has brought me nearer God,
Though oft it led through sorrow's gates.
Though not the way I'd choose,
In my way I might lose
The joy that yet for me awaits.

Not what I wish to be,
Nor where I wish to go,
For who am I that I should choose my way?
The Lord shall choose for me,
'Tis better far, I know,
So let him bid me go, or stay.

The cross that I must bear,
If I a crown would wear,
Is not the cross that I should take;
But, since on me 'tis laid,
I'll take it, unafraid,
And bear it for the Master's sake.

Submission to the will
Of him who guides me still
Is surety of his love revealed;
My soul shall rise above
This world in which I move;
I conquer only where I yield.

C. Austin Miles

NOTES

[1] "The Pastor's Sabbath," *Leadership* 6, no. 2 (Spring 1985): 55.
[2] Ibid., 56.

6

THE DIFFICULTY OF
KNOWING GOD

Hebrews 4:12–5:10

Susan was a vibrant, outgoing young woman from an almost pagan (the American version) background. She was even more attractive because of her simple, straightforward honesty. I had known her a couple of years when she announced to me that she and her boyfriend, Allen, had decided to live together. I was stunned.

She was a professing Christian, and her friend seemed an extraordinarily sensitive, caring young man. More from the role of father than pastor, I asked permission to talk with them about their choice. Why this choice, with all its problems? The answer was the standard one: "We love each other and want to be happy." Why then settle for a relationship that is guaranteed to end sooner or later, with certain unhappiness? Why not marry and build a lasting relationship on a solid commitment?

Allen's response reflected the prevailing consensus of urban young America. "I really love Susan, but how can I be sure that I will always love her, that she will love me? How can I make a permanent commitment with so many uncertainties? That would scare me to death!" It was no surprise to me to find him not the least interested in a relationship with God. In his fear of the risk of commitment without guarantee, he wrote off the possibility of any intimate relationship.

At the heart of an intimate relationship is a profound sense of safety. The rest of faith that our Hebrew brother tried to illustrate for us is precisely that kind of emotional, spiritual, and even psychological safety. We are safe with God. Nothing apart from God himself can touch us, and he seeks nothing but our best interests. Yet that kind of safe, intimate relationship with GOD is a terrible, awesome prospect!

"I want to know God" is one of the most audacious statements any human has ever uttered. The very idea of an intimate, loving relationship with a Being we cannot see or touch, whose thoughts determine our continued existence from one instant to the next is preposterous! How could I ever stand to get close to someone like him? We recoil from the possibility, and, for the sake of our own eternal salvation, try to settle for something considerably less than intimacy.

Far too many modern Christians opt out of intimacy with God by gutting the meaning of the idea of "relationship." This can be accomplished in several ways, I suppose, but there are two that seem most common. First, too many define a relationship with God as a merely legal arrangement. This legal link is set up something like this: I confess my sins to him and "accept Jesus as my Savior." By that decision, my name is instantly (and irrevocably, some would say) enrolled in the Book of Life, and I am born again.

This legal transaction, we believe, gives us all the relationship with God that we must have in order to get to heaven. But that sort of relationship is in the same league as my relationship with my health insurance company. There is protection, mutual obligation, and responsibility. It sounds almost as warm as détente, doesn't it? We pastors will deny it to the death, but that is the experience of a great many of the people who sit in our pews.

The other escape from intimacy with God is a warmer, emotional one. It is constructed much like the legal one, except that I cash in the emotional dimension of my personality. Having "accepted Jesus as my Savior," I now seek to "enjoy his presence." Any stirring of my emotions in a religious context is *de facto* evidence, irrefutable proof, of his presence. I can revel in my (positive) emotions. Whatever or whomever I can find to stir my religious emotions I use with abandon because this is the presence of God.

You may accuse me of being caustic and cynical. I do not intend to be either. I am convinced that I am much closer to an accurate evaluation of American evangelicals than I really want to be. And if I grieve for my own people, what must be going on in the heart of God?

I am not a mystic nor can I claim visions and revelations of any sort. I am a child of my age, burdened with an analytical intellect that balks at the uncommon or unusual. In the old classics of spirituality, I read accounts of saints who immersed themselves in the manifest glory of God. I read those accounts with tears in my eyes, a longing in my heart, and question marks as large as spaceships in my mind. For me, knowing God is a fearful, awesome, terrifying, contradictory, glorious prospect. Yet I am irresistibly drawn toward him.

Our Hebrew writer understood that between the believer and the rest of faith stood two mountains: human nature and God's nature. Let's explore these mountains one at a time.

TO KNOW GOD WE MUST FACE OURSELVES

Companionship with God is based squarely on simple honesty, and honesty is at a premium among fallen mortals. We are dishonest because the truth is too painful for us. We want to feel good about ourselves. We want to believe that we are good people, respectable people, godly and responsible people. We can convince ourselves that we are basically good so long as we don't get too close to God. But when he approaches, we begin to squirm.

Most Christians I know don't have much trouble with the idea of sinfulness as long as we talk about it theologically. But the honesty required in a relationship with God is something profoundly personal. We feel that we are in good company with a general confession such as "We are all sinners." But in the presence of God, I can say only, "Father, show me what I really am. I cannot see myself."

The Father's answer to that prayer comes to us through

the written Word of God. "The Word of God is living" (4:12). Scripture did not come to us through human choice nor through the art of a human author. It is living—God-breathed. But we must understand that God's Word is never separated from God himself. He did not give us a manuscript and leave us to make the best of it. In this Word we have the very presence of God. It is here that he comes to us and he speaks to us and reveals himself to us.

"For the Word of God is living and active." From this Greek word translated *active* comes our word "energy." It is energy; it is the power of God. In Scripture God energizes those who approach him. He enlightens, grips, transforms those who open themselves to him through his Word.

"It judges the thoughts and attitudes of the heart." *Judge* does not mean to pronounce a sentence, but to evaluate the evidence. In Scripture God evaluates us: attitudes, actions, motives, ambitions. He sees all the way through us. Of course, God knows all of this without any help anyway. But he uses the Word, which we can see and handle, to show us what is within us.

The apostle James uses an analogy that is helpful in understanding the importance of the Word of God to us. "Anyone who listens to the word but does not do what it says is like a man who looks at his face in a mirror and, after looking at himself, goes away and immediately forgets what he looks like" (1:23–24). Do you know anyone who gets up in the morning, looks in the mirror, says, "Oh, no, not again!" and walks away in order to forget what he looks like?

I could make Sam Walton, the billionaire owner of Wal-Mart stores, look like a pauper by comparison if I could invent a mirror that would make people actually look better the longer they spent studying their own faces in it. But this is precisely the kind of mirror that James describes. This living, active, penetrating, evaluating Word transforms the men and women who study themselves in its pages.

Here, then, is my dilemma. God draws me toward himself, but I am uncomfortable in his presence. He gives me his Word to reveal and purify me, but I cringe from the bitter truth. I know that there is no other way to my place of rest. But I hesitate, counting the terrible cost.

God will not hogtie us and drag us back to the mirror. He will never force us to gaze at the distorted image we find there until the mirror can do its work. His grace has brought us to that point. His grace will carry us further—if we permit. But his grace will never make that choice for us.

At this point grace confronts our will. Will we look long enough to be changed? The passing glance or forgetful gaze requires nothing of us. But the painful study that precedes the transformation requires personal commitment. That commitment is lived out in what we usually call the disciplines of spiritual life.

Discipline and grace do not mix easily. There is possibly no aspect of our relationship with God that is more frequently misunderstood. As a starting point for understanding, let's call these spiritual disciplines *the disciplines of availability*. These include (along with others) prayer, meditation, Bible reading and study, worship, and Christian fellowship.

The disciplines of availability are the same sort of declaration as the Sabbath rest, except that these declarations are made daily. The quarter or half hour deliberately carved out of a hectic schedule for Scripture and prayer may seem insignificant. The discipline required to do the carving may seem all out of proportion to the results. But we must make ourselves available. Many men and women fight to protect precious time with their families. Healthy marriages are built by couples who set time aside to invest in each other. Even prosperous businesses demonstrate that worthwhile relationships must be nurtured with regular, deliberately created time.

It is easy to fall into the trap of turning spiritual disciplines into duties. "You must read your Bible through every year and spend twenty minutes praying if you are to expect anything from God," says the Pharisee, wagging his finger in your face. But these disciplines of availability are simply nothing other than our response to the grace of God. He always takes the initiative. Paul made this clear in Philippians 2:12–13; Williams' translation is excellent: ". . . it is God Himself who is at work in you to help you desire it as well as do it."

I spend time with God because he is drawing me to himself. The effort it takes to discipline myself is a reflection of the finite and oh-so-present physical world in which I exist. The disciplines embody my choices to believe God rather than to listen to the unbelief of my senses, my clock, or my peers. They are my responsive "Yes" to the extended hand of grace. "Let us, therefore, make every effort to enter that rest, so that no one will fall by following [the Israelites'] example of disobedience" (Hebrews 4:11).

THE DISTANCE TO A HOLY GOD

Our discomfort in the presence of God's Word is not the only barrier to companionship with God. While we have real difficulty within ourselves, we have an incredible problem with God. Our Hebrew writer continues: "Nothing in all creation is hidden from God's sight. Everything is uncovered and laid bare before the eyes of him to whom we must give account" (4:13).

Awesome! How can I deal with a God like that? Two graphic words are here. The first, translated *uncovered* in the NIV (and *naked* in the KJV) means exactly that: "Without anything to cover." The second word comes from a military context. In hand-to-hand combat a soldier defeats his enemy. Standing above the slumped form, the victor grabs his enemy's head and pulls it back, exposing his neck to the sword in hand. His neck is "laid bare." He is totally at the mercy of the conqueror.

That is a truthful but frightening picture of our position before God. We are totally at his mercy. One thought, one word from almighty God and we cease to exist. Should he have a single momentary lapse of memory, all that has been created would instantaneously cease to exist. We are dealing with the Eternal God, not a benevolent big brother who pretends to ignore what he sees is wrong about us.

Isn't it terrifying to consider standing before a God from whom we can hide nothing? Not one thought, not one word, not one intention, not one hidden motive is overlooked. He is a

God from whom "no secrets are hid." We can hide nothing. All of our pretenses, our self-justifications, our rationalizations, and our carefully crafted explanations as to why we behave as we do simply evaporate when we step into the presence of God. How could any of us have an intimate relationship with a God like that? If we shy away from him because of our own sinfulness, how much more must we run from him because of his holiness?

But the plain truth is that we modern Christians are not awed by the character of God. There is little respect for him or understanding of his character among us. We take him for granted, using him as a crutch when we feel weak ourselves. We say we worship him, but our worship is usually rated on its entertainment value for us. We invoke his name over our plans, preparations, programs, and potlucks. We might admit that he is distant, but we blithely assume that when we approach those pearly gates, he will be overjoyed to see us coming.

We have become so blind to his character that we apparently believe that God has obligated himself to be at our beck and call. All we have to do is raise our hand or whisper a prayer and God is compelled to come and do whatever we want. He is almost like a genie in a magic bottle. We believe that he exists just to take care of us and our needs, to fill our lives with the good things we want. We ignore him and disregard his revealed will for our lives when it doesn't quite suit us. We go our own way doing our own thing, seeking our own satisfaction—until we get into trouble. Then we come running back and crying, "Oh, God, where were you when I needed you?"

Job may have lived before any of the Old Testament was written, but he understood much more about God than most of us. He realized that God was completely out of his league and that any contact between them would be disastrous for him. "He is not a man like me that I might answer him, that we might confront each other in court" (9:32). Though he had honored and served God with integrity, he feared him: "Then would I speak up without fear of him, but as it now stands with me, I cannot" (9:35). Job's deepest cry was for someone who could be the go-between for him with God: "If only there were someone to arbitrate between us, to lay his hand upon us both, someone to remove God's rod from me, so that his terror would frighten me no more" (9:33–34). God heard and answered that cry across the distance, not only for Job, but for you and me.

THE BRIDGE TO COMPANIONSHIP

If we as American Christians have a hard time with Sabbath rest, we have almost as much trouble with the idea of the priesthood. Our theological reasons for refusing to call ministers "priests" are sound and biblical. Instead, we believe that all Christians are priests, but you haven't studied many Sunday school lessons on that topic, have you? Perhaps it is one of those cases where that which is everyone's responsibility is actually no one's responsibility. Or, maybe . . . we don't need the priesthood because we are not awestruck with the majesty of God. We feel quite secure enough to come into his presence on our own.

God instituted the human priesthood to reveal his plan for the restoration of fellowship broken in the Garden of Eden. In that revelation he also revealed his own character. The writer summarizes the priestly office: God calls people to represent others before Himself. They must offer sacrifices for their own sins first, but because of their weaknesses, they can be compassionate (5:1–4).

But the human priesthood was not enough. Like every other man, the priest had to reckon with God on his own account. But there is one Priest, and only one, who can go into the presence of God pure and holy, and not take the blood of animals. It is his own blood that Jesus Christ carries into the presence of God for us. He is the go-between for whom Job longed. Being God, Jesus understands the burning purity of holiness. Being man, he understands our condition. He is the perfect Representative for us in the presence of God.

The writer in 5:5–10 probably had in mind Jesus' prayer in the Garden of Gethsemane where the Evangelists tell us that Jesus prayed in such agony that bloody sweat dripped from his face. In that garden, Jesus wrestled with the distance that existed between his Father and his friends. He felt that distance personally and from both sides. He carried the entire burden of that awful reality, the weight and guilt of the sin and suffering of the whole world. He carried it though the garden; he carried it to the cross. And he took his own blood into the presence of the Father on our behalf.

The distance between a holy God and us has been eliminated. As Adam and Eve walked with an unseen Presence in the breezes of the evening, we approach him in awe—yet in safety. Read these words as if you had never heard them before.

> Since we have a great high priest who has gone through the heavens, Jesus the Son of God, let us hold firmly to the faith we profess. For we do not have a high priest who is unable to sympathize with our weaknesses, but we have one who has been tempted in every way, just as we are—yet was without sin. Let us then approach the throne of grace with confidence, so that we may receive mercy and find grace to help us in our time of need.
>
> Hebrews 4:14–16

What more can my words add? I stand dumbstruck. I can enter the presence of God without fear! No longer must I try, futilely, to hide from him. As I approach him, I still shudder; but like a child with his father, I reach up and place my hand in the hand of Jesus, and the fear melts away. I am at home in my Father's house, and I find rest.

> Children of the heavenly Father
> Safely in his bosom gather;
> Nestling bird nor star in heaven
> Such a refuge e'er was given.
>
> God his own doth tend and nourish;
> In his holy courts they flourish.
> From all evil things he spares them;
> In his mighty arms he bears them.
>
> Neither life nor death shall ever
> From the Lord his children sever;
> Unto them his grace he showeth,
> And their sorrows all he knoweth.

Praise the Lord in joyful numbers,
   Your Protector never slumbers;
At the will of your Defender
   Every foeman must surrender.

Though he giveth or he taketh,
   God his children n'er forsaketh;
His the loving purpose solely
   To preserve them pure and holy.[1]

Caroline V. Sandell-Berg
Translated by Ernst
William Olson

NOTE

[1] Text translation by Caroline Sandell-Berg. Copyright © Board of Publication, Lutheran Church in America. Reprinted by permission of Augsburg Fortress.

7

MATURITY IS MORE THAN AGE

Hebrews 5:11–6:3, 9–12

I remember well the summer I thought I had grown up. When I was graduated from Bible college in the spring, my father gave me the old family station wagon. It was a drab white 1963 Ford Ranch Wagon. It looked massive and drove a lot like the USS *Missouri*. With a six-cylinder engine it was a hot car! I could accelerate from a standstill to sixty miles per hour in less than five minutes—when headed downhill! It was five years old, but I was proud, nonetheless. I was free and independent. I had a degree and a car, and I was ready to take on the world. I thought I had finally grown up. I had arrived.

I suppose that if young people knew how little they really understand when graduated from college, every one of them would suffer from severe clinical depression. But in the goodness of God it takes years to discover how little we know. In one sense, I am certain about much less than I was twenty years ago. There is so much less black and white and so much more grey. But of this I am certain: there is no place or time to stop living, learning, pondering, and stretching. These are the elements of maturity.

Woven into this epistle is the cardinal truth that Christians do not live in isolation from one another. Later, our responsibilities to one another will become very clear. But here we find the foundational principle of the church: every Christian is indeed a

priest, and the priest's efforts always turn outward toward those
around about. The doctrine of the priesthood of every believer
rests squarely on a clear understanding of Christian maturity.

IMMATURITY IS THE NORM

This letter was addressed to Christians who had been
believers for years. They had sat under the teachings of the
church (which, by the way, involved thoroughly catechizing
new converts). They had learned the facts about Christ: who he
was and what he came to do. But something was desperately
wrong. By this time, these believers should have developed
from care-receivers into care-givers. But they still required
pampering and bottles (5:11–13). They had nothing to give;
they were merely absorbing the loving efforts and conscientious
ministry of the fellowship. Consequently, they were in danger.

Verse 11 in the NASB reads, "You have become dull of
hearing," but the NIV reads "You are slow to learn." The first is
the more nearly accurate translation of the verb. These believers
had not always been hard of hearing. They had started off well
in their walk with Christ. But now their senses had become
blunted; their spiritual appetites had become poor; where once
they had begun to taste the meat of God's will, now they had
reverted to the baby bottle.

Too many of us believe that being faithful church
members is the same as being mature. Take a person who has
been a Christian for twenty years and has conscientiously
attended church for all those years. By virtue of seniority, we
assume maturity, don't we? Maturing Christians will be faithful
members of God's church, but there is nothing in church
attendance that assures maturity.

I will stick my neck out even further: in most churches,
there is little that even encourages maturity. Too many
Christians sit in the pews, recite the (informal!) rituals of
worship, serve on a committee where they demand their own
way, and expect the preacher and the officers to coddle and
burp them. Pastors and leaders are so anxious to maintain the
averages and the offerings that they broadcast a subliminal

message readily absorbed by the pew potatoes: "All God really expects of you is to attend and tithe. If you want to get involved, we can make room—we need volunteers in the nursery. But you don't need to do anything—you're okay!" Horse feathers and hens' teeth! What foolishness!

Before we can define Christian maturity, we must understand the difference between "milk" and "solid food." Jesus himself clarified the issue for us at the well in Samaria. The disciples were chiefly concerned about the growling of their stomachs, and paused only long enough to be surprised that Jesus bothered with that broken woman. "Rabbi, eat something," which, translated, means, "Hurry up and ask the blessing so we can eat."

And Jesus responded, "I have food to eat that you know nothing about. . . . My food is to do the will of him who sent me and to finish his work. Do you not say, 'Four months more and then the harvest'? I tell you, open your eyes and look at the fields! They are ripe for harvest" (John 4:32–35). The capacity for helping others is the difference between an infant sucking his bottle and the maturing believer who feasts on solid food.

Don't read me wrong here. I believe in babyhood! I love to be involved in nurture groups and discipleship groups for new converts. There is a freshness and vitality about new-found faith that renews for me again and again the wonder of forgiveness. Babyhood is a proper and necessary part of every biography. A tourist visiting a remote village in Scotland asked an old gentleman on the street, "Were any famous people born here?" The old fellow replied, "No. Only babies!" And I dare say that if we took better care of baby Christians in our churches, we would have far fewer problems down the road.

The problem among the Hebrews was not that they had been babies. They were now babies, but not ordinary babies. They might have been chronologically and intellectually mature, but they had withered into stunted, deformed, malnourished spiritual babies. They were only a shadow of what they had been. Once they had been outgoing and vibrant. Now they were turning in upon themselves. Once they had led the missionary campaign under the banner of Christ. Now they had circled the wagons and were busy keeping what they could for themselves.

The effects of institutionalized immaturity is devastating. When Christians are not challenged with the work of the kingdom, they occupy themselves with petty, personal, and political games. Can you show me a church that is splintered and divided over buildings, choirs, color schemes, orders of worship, styles of music, spiritual gifts, *ad nauseam*? I will show you a congregation that has settled for immaturity as the "normal" Christian condition. Once immaturity becomes acceptable in the Christian fellowship, it takes an act of God to shake things loose because stunted Christians will, like wounded boars, fight any challenge to their selfishly ingrown little worlds.

THE MARKS OF MATURITY

What does it mean to be mature? The first, easiest definition that comes to our minds is the legal one. Any American is legally an adult at eighteen years of age. Parents are no longer legally responsible for their offspring's behavior, debts, or necessities of life. An eighteen-year-old can vote, own property, drive and own a car, hold a job, run for public offices, get married, have children—without answering to anyone. But you and I both know very well that legal adulthood is not the same thing as maturity. In fact, it doesn't even mean that the eighteen-year-old is trying to mature.

Maturing is emotional and spiritual progress. It is a process in which we discover our uniqueness, our abilities, and our liabilities. Through these discoveries we learn how we differ from others, and how we are similar. And we gradually come to accept those differences and similarities as good and proper rather than as marks of inferiority. As believers, we learn who we are, why we are here, and how we fit into God's scheme of things.

For the Christian, maturation brings a sense of confidence. We grow more confident in ourselves as capable and worthwhile individuals. But more than that, we gain confidence in our relationship with God. The conviction grows trial by trial that he is who he claims to be; that he does what he promises to do; that he is in fact (not just in theory) involved intimately in the ordinary processes of our lives.

However, no believer matures by seeking that confidence. We accomplish nothing by searching for greater confidence or stronger faith (Oh, dear, where will I find my daily dose today?), or by praying and asking God for it (Dear God, give me faith!). This maturing confidence comes only as a by-product of service to God and our neighbor. It grows solely in the hearts of those who seek to serve God. It comes to those who learn to give, who invest time and effort in the lives and trials of their companions.

The first steps in doing God's work are tentative and halting. Fear, shame, self-doubt, and failure lurk at every opportunity. But—wonder of wonders—we discover that our fumbling efforts really do make a difference. In this we see the hand of God. Paul expressed the reality of this growing confidence: "Such confidence as this is ours through Christ before God. Not that we are competent in ourselves to claim anything for ourselves, but our competence comes from God. *He has made us competent as ministers* of a new covenant—not of the letter but of the Spirit; for the letter kills, but the Spirit gives life" (2 Cor. 3:4–6, emphasis mine).

At best, the idea of maturing is vague and impersonal. We find many good qualities in mature people, but I have chosen four that will provide us with a context in which to understand maturity. I am tempted to insert a batch of disclaimers because no four words will adequately summarize maturity. But let's start with these: Integrity, Sensitivity, Perseverance, and Teachableness.

> *Integrity* means that:
> —I am the same on the inside as I am on the outside. If observers could read my motives, they would find no deliberate discrepancies between my inner attitudes and my outward professions.
> —I am learning to speak the truth in love, tactfully.

—I am willing to confront problems even when it would be easier to ignore them.
—I keep my word and fulfill my commitments.
—I shoulder responsibility for the consequences of my actions when I am tempted to shove the blame toward another.
—I refuse to be partial to the influential and wealthy, neglecting the weak and poor.

Sensitivity means that:
—I am willing—and able—to put myself in other people's shoes.
—I try to spot needs and opportunities to help before crises erupt.
—I will bear the pain of a friend, when with all my heart I want to distance myself from it.
—I choose freely to release my just rights and privileges if it appears that I can remove a barrier between my neighbor and God.
—I will listen with my ears, my face, my eyes, and my heart, and will wait to give advice until I feel the hurt of my friend.

Perseverance means that:
—I take a dim view of quitting.
—I will seek the help and counsel of others when I am discouraged or frustrated.
—I approach my responsibilities with the understanding that all that I do is only a tiny part of what God is doing. I may or may not see the success or satisfaction that I want. But I stay put until God moves me.
—I expect to face opposition and difficulty from surprising sources, and, when it comes, I press on one step at a time.
—I can afford to be patient with others. God did not, overnight, make me what I have become, and I cannot demand hasty changes in my companions and fellow workers.

—I keep my dreams alive, for God is at work.

Teachableness means that:

—I will swallow my pride and admit that there is always someone who knows more than I do.

—I expect to learn from other people, especially those who disagree with me, criticize me, achieve more than I have, or outshine me at my best.

—I am willing to appear stupid to avoid making mistakes that might discredit me or my Savior.

—I do not have to be right to be happy, and I freely own up to my errors and poor judgment because I learn from failure as well as success.

—I know God is bigger than my narrow experience and limited knowledge, and that he has charming surprises waiting for me in the most unlikely places and people.

THE STEPS TO MATURITY

The writer of Hebrews gives us several steps that will lead us toward maturity. The first is in 6:1: "Let us go on to maturity." We think of the process of maturity as hard work. We struggle with our problems and through our trials. And it seems that the writer here is exhorting us to work harder! "Go on!" "Press on!" (NASB) But though this verb is translated in the active voice, it is actually in the passive voice. The literal translation is, "Let us be borne or carried on to maturity."

This is an entirely different point of view. God wants maturing children more than any of us parents want maturity for our children. The whole structure and rationale for the church (as God intended it to be) focuses on leading Christians toward maturity. When we let God have his way in our lives, it is as if we raise the sails and the wind of the Holy Spirit carries us forward. It can be rough going, and we sail through fierce storms. The wind is behind us, but the waves are in front and all around. We can't see ahead. We don't know what the next wave is going to do. But we can allow ourselves to be carried on through the storm by the wind of God in our sails. We can decide to let God do with us as he pleases. And we begin to mature.

The second step is in the clause *you have helped his people and continue to help them* (6:10). Some had fallen away, and many more were wavering and in danger. But the church still had a hope, an opportunity of again becoming what God intended. That hope rested on the loving pastoral care that they gave to one another. I have said it before at least twice, and I am going to say it again: Until Christians get involved in ministry to others, there can be no maturity. Period. Maturing means getting involved in the work of God's kingdom.

The work of the kingdom always involves caring for people. It might mean a Sunday school class—and every class member becomes your spiritual ward. It might be a Bible club in your home or gathering neighborhood teens for sports. It might mean visiting the local nursing home, and caring for a stranger as you would your parent. It might mean helping in an inner-city mission, or answering phones for the Crisis Pregnancy Center. It might mean faithfully and lovingly witnessing to neighbors and friends. It might mean working in the church office (I know a lot of pastors who desperately need loving hands to ease the load of administrative work). There are scores of ways that we help people in Jesus' name. But until we do, we cannot grow as Christians.

The third step is in the command *imitate those who through faith and patience inherit what has been promised* (6:12, emphasis mine). Imitate! Follow! Whom do you know who is walking with God? Father, mother, a friend at church? Deliberately pattern yourself after the strong points of their lives. Talk to them. Ask them to pray with you. Call them and ask their advice when you have decisions to make, even on matters about which you are sure. Talk to them when you get discouraged with what you are doing. Find out how they relate to God. Listen to their counsel. We become like the people who surround us. If we are going to grow up and serve God, we must surround ourselves with God's people: people who are growing, learning, challenging their own limitations and weaknesses.

But there is one more thing that I must say to be faithful to God's Word. I have skipped two paragraphs in this passage that form the downside choice. If we refuse to let God do his work of maturing us, we revert to stunted infancy. What then? Our brother makes it plain: "It is impossible for those who have once been enlightened . . . if they fall away, to be brought back to repentance." What awful danger we court when we thwart the work of God in our lives!

> Father, I know that all my life
> Is portioned out for me,
> And the changes that are sure to come
> I do not fear to see;
> But I ask thee for a present mind
> Intent on pleasing thee.
>
> I ask thee for a thoughtful love,
> Through constant watching wise,
> To meet the glad with joyful smiles,
> And wipe the weeping eyes;
> And a heart at leisure from itself
> To soothe and sympathize.
>
> Wherever in the world I am,
> In whatsoe'er estate,
> I have a fellowship with hearts
> To keep and cultivate,
> And a work of lowly love to do
> For the Lord on whom I wait.
>
> I ask thee for the daily strength
> To none that ask denied,
> And a mind to blend with outward life,
> Still keeping at thy side,
> Content to fill a little space
> If thou be glorified.
>
> In a service which thy will appoints
> There are no bonds for me;
> For my inmost soul is taught the truth
> That makes thy children free;
> And a life of self-renouncing love
> Is a life of liberty.
>
> Anna Laetitia Waring

8

THOSE INEVITABLE CONSEQUENCES

Hebrews 6:4–8; 10:26–31

Real choices result in real consequences. Choices that make no difference in final results are not real choices. They are pretexts arranged to give the appearance of freedom where there is none. I find in the epistle to the Hebrews (as in other parts of Scripture) a clear thesis that God does grant us the opportunity to make real choices with eternal consequences. If God enables real choices, then real consequences follow. We glory in the possibility of choosing the companionship of almighty God through his initiatives of grace. But if we can choose to respond, then we must also be able to choose to reject.

The two passages of Hebrews that form the basis for this chapter are explicit statements of the real consequences of a free choice to reject the grace of God. They are parallel passages in some aspects, yet they have a different impact. It may well be that each passage was addressed to a different group within the Hebrew church.

The first warning reads, "It is impossible for those who have once been enlightened . . . if they fall away, to be brought back to repentance" (6:4, 6). The second reads, "If we deliberately keep on sinning after we have received the knowledge of the truth, no sacrifice for sins is left" (10:26).

These are solemn words, and we must allow our Hebrew author to answer six crucial questions, if we are to understand these passages. I'll list them so that we will know the outline of our study:

1. Is it possible to fall away from God?

2. Who are these people who have fallen away from God?

3. What does it mean to fall away from God?

4. Why is repentance not possible for those who have fallen away?

5. Are those who have fallen away eternally lost?

6. What kind of relationship do we have with God?

IS IT POSSIBLE TO FALL AWAY FROM GOD?

Note that each of these warnings is phrased as a conditional clause, using the introductory word *if.* A conditional clause offers an alternative or it poses a hypothetical situation. A conditional clause does not state facts.

There is a mistranslation here: no *if* appears in the first passage. In adding the *if* and making this a conditional clause, the NIV follows the KJV to a point. In addition to adding the *if,* the KJV also translates the verb in the future tense: "If they shall fall away." This tends to create the idea of a hypothetical situation that exists only in the remote future. But this is not the literal translation of the phrase, and in this case the literal translation makes perfectly good sense.

The verb is actually a participle that emphasizes a completed event rather than a continuing process. The NASB gives the best translation: "and then have fallen away." The obvious intention of the writer was to state a fact: Some person or persons in his own time and experience had apparently fallen away. This is neither a hypothetical situation nor a rhetorical question. He knew of some who had fallen, and he wrote as if he expected his readers to be aware of the same fact. Our Hebrew brother would answer the first question, "Yes, it is possible; some already have."

The second passage, however, is built around a conditional clause. The writer uses the word *if.* He is not now stating facts; he is explaining the consequences of the alternatives we have. We can choose to continue to sin and fall under the judgment of the living God. Or, by implication, we can choose to quit sinning and avoid that awful fate.

But even here there is confusion in the minds of many Christians. "After all," we hear from pulpits and Christian radio and television, "we cannot avoid sinning every day in thought, word, and deed." The writer of Hebrews has a word—just one word—for those who are confused. That word is *deliberately*.

If we define sin to include every departure from the perfection of God, then mistakes, misunderstandings, and ignorance are sin. But we cannot avoid such shortcomings nor even know when we are falling into them. If we say that forgetfulness is a sin like adultery or bank robbery, we actually destroy the meaning of the word *sin*. You and I cannot avoid making mistakes, but we can avoid robbing a bank or running off with our neighbor's spouse. There is a distinct difference between a mistake and a sin, and the difference lies here in this word *deliberately*.

The basic biblical definition of sin is "the deliberate transgression of the known will of God" (1 John 3:4). The sin that the writer of Hebrews is talking about here is not the mistakes of fallen humanity, but the deliberate doing of those things we know to be wrong.

WHO ARE THESE PEOPLE WHO HAVE FALLEN AWAY FROM GOD?

Four parallel phrases in 6:4–8 describe those who fall away. Our author uses not one but four, as if he wanted to leave no doubt as to the kind of people who had fallen away. Three of the verbs have explicit meanings.

The first phrase is *who have once been enlightened*. The word *enlightened* is often translated in the New Testament, *to teach* or *to instruct*. The early church placed heavy emphasis on teaching new converts the principles of their new faith. In one of the earliest church buildings known (Church of St. John in

Jerusalem), a separate area divided from the sanctuary by a half-height wall was reserved for those under instruction. At the conclusion of this catechism, which lasted months or even years, the new converts were baptized.

These who had fallen away were individuals who had already come into the church through the ordinary steps of conversion. They had taken at least the first steps in the Christian faith.

Those who want to argue that these fallen ones had never been true Christians settle on the word *taste* , in the second and fourth phrases, to prove their case. "To taste," it is argued, "means to touch to the tip of the tongue, as if to find out whether it is sweet or sour." But the word is used only one other time in the New Testament. That is in Hebrews 2:9: "But we see Jesus, who was made a little lower than the angels, now crowned with glory and honor because he suffered death, so that by the grace of God he might taste death for everyone."

Taste death is the same verb as *tasted the heavenly gift,* and *tasted the goodness of the word.* Did Jesus just brush close to death in order to give the appearance that he had died? Our whole system of salvation is based on the fact that Jesus really died. And in his death he carried the penalty of all our sins. He took it as his own, in all its pain, and all its terror, and all its evil. If that is the way Jesus tasted death, then these people had also tasted of the good things of God fully in all its power and glory.

If we take the plain meaning of these verbs, individually as well as together, we hear our writer's answer to the second question: these who had fallen away had once been truly and fully Christian.

The phrasing of the second warning, however, suggests that the writer was not talking about the same group of people. The verb *keep on sinning* does not imply a return to sin, as the idea of *falling away* does. These persons were probably members of that sympathetic fringe of people around the church who acknowledged that the Gospel was attractive yet refused to yield fully to its demands. These hangers-on continued to live in sin while giving mental assent to the Gospel. The church has always attracted some such half-way Christians. But this warning comes from the writer's heart. As far as the judgment of God was concerned, these sympathetic nonbelievers were actually compounding their own guilt.

The two passages, then, give the same message to two different groups of people. Both had experienced the initiatives of grace in their lives, and both had begun to reject those initiatives. Both faced the same consequences for their rejection.

WHAT DOES IT MEAN TO FALL AWAY FROM GOD?

The word we usually use for these who have fallen away is *apostate*. According to *Nelson's Illustrated Bible Dictionary*, "apostasy is generally defined as the determined, willful rejection of Christ and his teachings by a Christian believer."[1] Apostates repudiate all interest in and all knowledge of God. They might laugh at and ridicule what others consider sacred, or they might persecute Christians who come in contact with them. They may take pride in their sins, and actively encourage others to join them in deliberately profane mockery.

One example in Scripture is King Saul, who hunted David out of pure jealousy—and with hardly a pang of conscience. Another is Judas, who ended his life in a dark remorse untouched by even a faint ray of hope in the mercy of God. These people—I believe that their number is not large—have abandoned not only their faith in God but their respect for God. For them, there is nothing, absolutely nothing, about God that is attractive.

We must be clear about one thing: A vast difference distinguishes backsliding from apostasy. It is true that a person must backslide before falling into apostasy. Apostasy is the final condition of total hardening. But backsliding and apostasy are not the same.

Most Christians I know can recall times when they have pulled away from God or grown negligent and disinterested. This is backsliding. Backslidden Christians may become involved in even the grossest sin. But there remains in the heart a hidden attraction to God. Backsliders know that things are not as they once were, and there is a secret sorrow. God seems distant, with great barriers in the way, but there is also a buried longing to come back. For all who choose to return, the path to God is open, and inviting. The door of repentance leads back to fellowship with God. But for the apostate, there is no longer any drawing toward God.

WHY IS REPENTANCE NOT POSSIBLE FOR THOSE WHO HAVE FALLEN AWAY?

The final three phrases in the paragraph explain why repentance is impossible. "Impossible to be brought back to repentance" is a passive phrase, suggesting that the apostate cannot be compelled to return. We cannot force him; God will not. But the impossibility lies not with a decree of God (remember that old gospel song about crossing that invisible line?) but with the choices of the apostate himself.

The last two verbs in the paragraph are *are crucifying* the Son and *subjecting* him to public disgrace. These verbs are in the present tense. The verse could properly be translated "It is impossible for those . . . to be brought back to repentance . . . while they are crucifying the Son of God all over again and while they are subjecting him to public disgrace." Again, the verbs throw the burden of rebellion onto the shoulders of the rebels. There is, perhaps, a point at which God gives up on the hardened apostate, though I doubt it. It is the individual who does the repudiating, not God.

Apostasy is a moral kind of impaired hearing. Whenever we neglect to listen and respond to the voice of God, we begin to harden. We are then less able to hear him the next time, and the next. Our God of grace may step up the volume from time to time, but if hardening continues, we will finally be morally stone deaf. Our condition is neither God's doing nor his fault; it is ours. His grace has encountered our rebellion, and he will not overpower us.

This fact is vividly expressed in the second passage: "No sacrifice for sins is left." But the key is the verb: "if we deliberately keep on sinning." It is a present participle, implying continuing action. Our writer obviously does not refer to a single act of disobedience. This warning concerns a life of sinning, a lifestyle that is characterized by disobedience.

If God does not arbitrarily cut anyone off, there is a point beyond which he will not go. That point is the violation of the human will. There is no sacrifice that will save a person who *will not* be saved. It is not that Christ's sacrifice was not sufficient. Christ died once, a perfect man who paid the penalty for the sins of every man and woman who ever lived. But that complete atonement will not save a person who deliberately continues a lifestyle of sin and disobedience. But more on this when we look for the answer to the last question.

ARE THOSE WHO HAVE FALLEN AWAY ETERNALLY LOST?

Most of us evangelicals do not have a problem with the warning in our second passage that God will judge the nonbeliever. But what about the apostate? The writer of the epistle does not state explicitly that apostate persons are eternally lost. Rather, by using an analogy from farming, he points out to us the logical outcome. Rain (God's grace) falls on all fields equally. The productive field is used and cared for; the unproductive, worthless field is cursed and ultimately burned.

Obviously the analogy is not perfect in every detail, for even fruitful fields are burned over once in a while to rid the soil of weed seed. *Burning* here is the opposite of blessing, and its obvious sense in this passage is destruction. There are two choices: response and rejection. Each has its own inevitable consequence: blessing or burning. As long as the pattern of responses continues, the consequences are unchanged.

If those who have fallen away are in the end forceably reclaimed by the sovereign power of God, then the passage as a whole is pointless. True, apostate people do great damage to God's work on earth. But in the scales of cosmic importance, what happens here in these few years is all but pointless, if there are no eternal consequences. God would not have inspired the writer of Hebrews to write such carefully crafted warnings if, in fact, the warnings were ultimately unnecessary. Christians can break off their relationship with God and become hard and deaf. If they persist in rejecting the grace of God until death overtakes them, they share the fate of those who never submitted to his lordship at all.

WHAT KIND OF RELATIONSHIP DO WE HAVE WITH GOD?

An analogy is a comparison that explains a difficult reality by describing something familiar. Many of Jesus' parables were analogies, such as the sower and the seed. He was using an analogy when he called himself the Good Shepherd. Each analogy explained something about the spiritual world through word pictures drawn from our world. Every analogy is limited because nothing in our world strictly parallels the spiritual world. We must learn to recognize the limits of every analogy.

The Scriptures use many kinds of analogies to describe our relationship with God. One particular analogy has come to be almost exclusively utilized by American evangelicals. It is based on Paul's use of legal terms to explain salvation: "Therefore being justified by faith" and "the works of the law" bring to our minds a picture of a heavenly courtroom. God is the Judge and we are in the dock, on trial for our lives. The charge? Rebellion. All appears lost until Jesus approaches the bar and pleads the mercy of the court on our behalf. He has already paid the penalty for our sin: death. If we accept him by faith as our substitute, his holiness covers our sin. The penalty has been paid, and the Judge can declare us not guilty.

By such a legal transaction, we sinners are declared righteous, and our names are entered into the Book of Life. We are saved by no effort of our own. But there are limitations to this legal analogy that we do not always understand. While this might be an accurate picture of one aspect of salvation, it is wrong if carried too far. From a court of law we receive a legal decree that grants us the privileges that we sought. That decree is now ours, and we use those privileges independently of the judge who granted them. That is not how God works out his plan of salvation in our lives.

Another analogy is needed to explain how the work of salvation is carried on in us. Jesus gave us one that best balances Paul's legal analogy (and Paul himself used other analogies also).

> "I am the true vine, and my Father is the gardener . . . If a man remains in me and I in him, he will bear much fruit; apart from me you can do nothing. If anyone does not remain in me, he is like a branch that is thrown away and withers; such branches are picked up, thrown into the fire and burned" (John 15:1, 5–6).

The branch is living and fruitful only as long as it is connected to the vine. From the vine comes nourishment, strength, water—in fact, life itself. The branch does not earn its place. The relationship is a natural, growing one. We branches have a choice about whether we are going to stay attached to the vine and whether the life-giving sap is going to continue to flow through us into the fruit of our lives. This is radically different from the world of legal standing. Jesus is talking about a continuing, life-giving relationship with himself.

If we believe that our salvation is based upon a one-time legal transaction, then we will tend to rest on that decree and neglect the continuing relationship. That is the situation of vast numbers of American evangelicals. By explaining salvation almost exclusively through the legal analogy, we have been guilty of distorting the Gospel of Jesus Christ. God did not create a plan of redemption just to *save* us: our personal salvation is only part of God's whole plan. The ultimate purpose in the heart and mind of God is to restore the fellowship, the relationship, the companionship that was broken by Adam and Eve in the garden.

If we look at our warning passage in Hebrews through the analogy of relationship, the pieces fall into place. In fact, Jesus himself said exactly the same thing that our Hebrew author said: those who choose to reject the initiatives of grace eventually cut themselves off from life. It may be unsettling for some to learn that our probationary period does not end in a single religious experience. On the other hand, we also learn that the whole point of God's work in this world is to have a continuing, growing, intimate, and individual friendship with every person who will respond to his offer. There are so many glorious possibilities in companionship with almighty God that the idea of continuing probation doesn't bother me so much. How about you?

> O Lamb of God, still keep me
> Close to thy piercèd side
> 'Tis only there in safety
> And peace I can abide.
> What foes and snares surround me,
> What lusts and fears within!
> The grace that sought and found me
> Alone can keep me clean.
>
> 'Tis only in thee hiding
> I feel myself secure;
> Only in thee abiding,
> The conflict can endure.
> Thine arm the victory gaineth
> O'er every hateful foe;
> Thy love my heart sustaineth
> In all its cares and woe.
>
> James George Deck

NOTE

[1] *Nelson's Illustrated Bible Dictionary,* ed. Herbert Lockyer, Sr. (Nashville: Thomas Nelson, 1986), 78.

9

GOD TAMPERS WITH
SACRED THINGS

Hebrews 6:13–10:18

Relax! I am not going to wade through five chapters at
once. Perhaps I should include at this point the full text of
Hebrews 6–10, but I won't. You would skip over it anyway,
wouldn't you? This is the heart of the epistle to the Hebrews,
and it means next to nothing to many of us. We may
understand theoretically how important the priesthood of
Christ is. But since the priesthood itself is meaningless in this
twentieth century, we look elsewhere for analogies that move
our hearts.

But before we skip these chapters, let's look at the broader
context. We can find here a lesson that too many American
evangelicals (may I include those who claim the label "funda-
mentalist" also?) need to learn. It is this: companionship with a
creative God is a life filled with both serendipity and confound-
ing changes. God simply will not leave things as they are. And
that, for many of us, is unnerving.

Some years ago a friend and I, as pastor and layman, were
discussing plans and hopes for our congregation. Alex had
retired from a successful career as a chemical engineer. He had
been a part of the Green Revolution, the application of chemical
technology to Third-World agriculture and had traveled worldwide. I knew that we differed on many points, and I was glad

when he began to tell me his feelings about what our church ought to be.

My own feelings changed, however, as the image he painted took shape in my mind. What emerged was not an evangelistic church with city-wide impact nor a missionary church with worldwide vision. He did not describe even an active suburban church, but he drew a picture of the little country church in which he had grown up. His dreams were wrapped up in nostalgia for the social community that had revolved around the rural church house of half a century past. This, for him, was "historic Christianity." He wanted to bring back what had been lost and relive those days.

He could not see, however, that much of the Methodism of his childhood was already spiritually hollow. It had long since lost a good deal of the fire and vigor of the Wesleys, Francis Asbury, and others who had spread scriptural holiness around the world. Mesmerized by the past, he was unwilling (unable?) to accept the fact that the future could be better than the past. In fact, he looked me straight in the eye some time later and told me with conviction that he had not changed a single idea since he was graduated from college.

Tragic. Change was an enemy that was to be fought like the devil. But how can unbending men and women walk in close companionship with a God who changes things? Each time God acts, he acts in a creative way. He is never programmed by the past nor confined by our narrow options. He is always trying to show us more and lead us deeper. Our Hebrew brother was writing to a group of Christians who had come to fear change passionately. What can believers do when God tampers with sacred things?

THE SACRED WORLD OF TEMPLE WORSHIP

Our author began with a simple description of the furnishings and ceremony of temple worship—an intensely familiar picture to these Jewish Christians—more than that—it was a sacred picture (9:1–7). The tabernacle, and later the temple, were sacred places, but it was the institution of the priesthood that was the center of attention as our Hebrew author unfolds the work of Christ. God had chosen to set apart the sons of Aaron. They were to be God's representatives. Only they could take the sinner's offering into the presence of God. Only they could speak for God and pronounce God's blessing to the waiting worshiper. How important it was for them to be there. Without them, how could anyone approach God?

Jewish believers in the Christian church faced a serious problem. Since infancy, they had been brought up to value the work of the priesthood and to honor it. This was God's plan—the way God had ordained that we should worship him. And the Jews around the world prided themselves on their temple and their priesthood and their access to God through it.

But when Jesus came, all that changed. This radical change was not immediately apparent because Jesus and all his disciples were Jewish, and devoutly so. Not until the appearance of Paul and his mission to the Gentiles did the threat to the Jews' sacred system become clear. Non-Jews could become believers and enjoy all the privileges of the faith without accepting any of the Jewish system. In only a few years, there were more Gentile Christians than Jewish. For the staunch conservatives the problem seemed to be the abandonment of the law of God. But for many others, there was the gnawing question, "Has God really tampered with the sacred things? Are we losing something exquisitely valuable?"

This was no small problem. In fact, it was a wrenching dilemma. When the Jews looked back on their history, they looked all the way back to a face-to-face meeting between God and Moses there on the mountain. Moses received the law from the mouth of God. The instructions for the tabernacle, the priesthood, and the sacrificial system came from God himself.

The whole of Jewish history was a long struggle between God and the rebellious nation. Again and again judgment came because of idolatry. Customs of surrounding nations infiltrated the culture of God's people and corrupted them time after time. Finally they were exiled for their stubborn rebellion, taken from the land that God had given, and settled far away. Would they ever learn the lesson God was trying to teach them?

Yes! The remnant returned to rebuild the temple and reestablish the worship of Yahweh. They still stumbled at times, but gradually came a shared conviction that they were going to obey God. The law of God became the law of the nation, deliberately and consciously. The Sabbath was observed religiously. The commandments of God were explained and expanded by generation after generation of rabbis. Yes! They were God's people and proud of it. They might have to fight for their faith, but fight they would, and that to the death!

But just at the point at which they had learned the lesson to take God's law seriously, God seemed to change everything. And, tragically, those who were most earnest in defending the law of God did not even recognize him standing in their midst!

OUT OF THE SHADOWS INTO THE REALITY

The error into which the Jews had fallen in their earnest defense of the truth of God is a common and dangerous one. They had confused the means with the end.

Our Hebrew teacher painted a word picture in chapter 9: the sanctuary, the priest, the altar, the sacrifice, the Most Holy Place. These were all ordinary, material things. The sanctuary was made of wood and leather and fabric, materials used every day in ordinary life. The priest was an ordinary man called by God to do a job. That sacrifice was nothing unusual either. It was only an animal, the best of the flock, without defect or blemish; but only an animal like millions of others that roamed the pastures of the world. These sacred things were nothing in themselves. They were nothing but poor copies or flitting shadows of some great reality beyond the reach of human understanding. This the Jews had forgotten. In fact, three times our brother calls these sacred things *shadows* (8:5; 9:23; 10:1)!

The problem was not that the nation had forgotten about the coming of the Messiah. Absolutely not. But they had forgotten that all the rituals, ceremonies, laws, and regulations were meaningless apart from the promise that Messiah would come. He would take away sin, not by the blood of these animals, but by a better sacrifice that would never have to be

repeated. He would give *himself!* He would be a priest who
would not have to atone for his own sin. He would never sleep
nor die nor go away so that the temporary service of stand-ins
would then be unnecessary.

The Jews had confused the end with the means. They had
forgotten why God gave the law and the priesthood. God gave
them the law to prepare them for the coming of Jesus Christ. It
was to be the schoolmaster, wrote Paul, that would lead them
to the Messiah. But they had come to believe that these sacred
things were ends in themselves to be used to please God. They
blindly maintained the forms, ignorant of the truth God was
actually trying to teach them. Jesus was the end and the
fulfillment of the Old Testament. That long and poignant
history was a lesson designed to teach them to recognize Jesus
when he came. He was the Reality to the dream.

Why did God use shadows and copies? Here we confront
the awful narrowness of our condition. We accept that which
we can touch and see as real. We easily dismiss that which we
cannot handle as unreal. The truth is that we have it exactly
reversed. All that we can touch and taste are temporary and
transient. It is the world we cannot see or touch that is real and
permanent. Down in the human personality may be a longing
for contact with a higher world. Philosophers and theologians
have tried to pin it down. But this is certain: the spiritual world
seems unreal because we have no way of visualizing what we
have never seen.

Therefore, God used tangible things and visible people to
persuade us that there is a greater reality. He told us again and
again that every one of these shadows pointed to the Reality
that was to come. Each type shed only a little light, but even
then it was more than most of the people could grasp. And
without the long history of shadows, no one—not one single
person—would ever have recognized Jesus. The ceremonies
repeated endlessly, the prophecies voiced century after century,
the priests consecrated generation after generation: every one of
these was necessary so that even a few could recognize what
was truly real.

WRAPPED UP IN SACRED THINGS

Sometimes God has to tamper with sacred things in order to force us to separate the shadows from the Reality. He must wrest our attention from the means and onto the End.

Let's take the printed Bible for an example. Only in the last four centuries have we had Scripture available to us in this way. We have come to hold the book itself to be sacred. On the front is stamped "Holy Bible." We give it a place of honor in our homes—the big family Bible on the coffee table. We encourage our children to carry their Bibles to church and we carry ours. I remember the pledge of allegiance to the Bible in vacation Bible school. I was also taught never to lay any other book on top of my Bible. Some have even made the King James Version sacred in itself, thinking that guarding this particular translation is protecting the sacred.

But is the Bible a means or an end? Is its value in what it is or where it points? In a Christmas play presented by our youth fellowship, the group was supposed to choose symbols to represent key parts of the Christmas story. A newspaper stood for the decree, because that is the way we learn the details of government today. A telephone was chosen to represent the angels, because they were the instruments through which God sent a message. And they chose the Bible to represent the manger. It was in the manger that the shepherds found Jesus, and it is in the Bible that we find Christ today.

What is the point of Scripture, apart from the central fact that it points to Jesus Christ? Reading the Bible is not a magic ritual. We must see Jesus in these pages; we must meet him here. We will never meet him anywhere else. The Scriptures are a means to find fellowship with God. He stands beyond the inspired book, waiting to reveal himself to us.

We can confuse the means with the end in every aspect of our life with God. Biblical tithing, as our author points out in 7:1–10, is the response of a grateful person in fellowship with a bountiful God. It is not a way to make a deal nor the payment of premiums on some sort of cosmic insurance policy. Prayer is companionship with God, the reverent sharing of our thoughts, dreams, needs, and friends with God. It is not the repetition of formulas or phrases to manipulate God.

I once asked a missionary friend on furlough from a third-world country about the use of discipleship-training programs with new converts. I was expecting to learn something fresh from the front lines. After all, my friend was seeing more conversions in a week than I was seeing in a year. But his answer stopped me cold. "We cannot recommend or even suggest any sort of uniform program like that. Our national pastors would misrepresent it. They would automatically assume that if they pushed people through the program, they would have done discipleship training." We Americans are not so blatant about it—just more hypocritical!

Even in our witnessing we sometimes confuse the end with the means. I counseled with a young drug addict who assured me that he wanted off drugs. I explained the plan of salvation, and his response to the sinner's prayer was revealing. "I've said these words before, but nothing ever happened!" We had given him the formula as if it were the end. And he had been disappointed. All of these good things—sacred things—must point directly to Jesus, who waits to make contact with us. If there is no relationship, our sacred things are meaningless.

In 1988 a Gallup Poll entitled *The Unchurched American: 10 Years Later* revealed some startling facts. While forty-four percent of those interviewed were unchurched, Gallup noted that "the unchurched are becoming increasingly receptive to what churches have to offer, and are staying away primarily out of inconvenience, not hostility." Sixty-three percent believe the Bible is God's Word, and seventy-seven percent say they pray, while seventy-two percent believe in the deity of Christ. Gallup's conclusion: "These people are ripe for the picking, but it will take new and creative strategies to reach them."[1]

I can imagine the hue and cry that will arise if anyone suggests "new strategies" in many evangelical churches! What about different times for worship or classes located away from the church? New styles of music or different kinds of musicians? Chairs in circles rather than pews in stubborn rows? Children's clubs instead of Sunday school? Home Bible studies in the place of Wednesday "prayer meetings"? Not to speak of lunch-hour Bible studies or friendship evangelism.

God may well challenge us to change some of the ways we worship him. He might lead us to change the way our churches are organized. He could lead us to adopt new methods and new practices and new rituals. He might ask us to get involved in ministries that we think of as more secular than sacred. What is our response? Do we find our security in having things just the way they have always been? Do we find it impossible to sense the presence of God when the rituals are different? We may have confused the means and the end.

I was reared in a conservative evangelical home, and began my college education in an equally conservative Bible school. In that tradition I had learned that "formal" churches were dead and "informal" churches were alive. I had an inquisitive mind, but few opportunities to visit "formal" services to see for myself how bad it was there. But I finally attended one in 1975. I was a short-term student at the Institute of Holy Land Studies in Jerusalem. The rest of my class went to the Garden Tomb for Sunday services, as did almost all American visitors. There the setting was inspirational—and "informal."

But I decided to go AWOL and visit St. Andrews. I was 10,000 miles away from home and no one would ever find out. St. Andrews is the Jerusalem congregation of the Church of Scotland, and the Scottish kirk is as "formal" as they come. The liturgy has survived almost unchanged for centuries. I ordered the butterflies in my stomach to hush their nonsense as I approached the huge oak doors and stepped inside, cautiously exploring this fearful new world.

With the force of a physical blow, I met the presence of God on the other side of that door! I was stunned! I could not participate fully in the service because I couldn't find my way through the service book. But never mind. I sensed that for these expatriate Christians, the ancient words of the liturgy were as living as anything I had ever heard in the churches I grew up in. I returned for five more services, and each time I met God in the liturgy and hymnody of the Church of Scotland.

The changes that our creative God may bring into our lives and our churches may be threatening at times. But I choose to find my hope and security in a God who does not change.

> Teach me thy way, O Lord, teach me thy way!
> Thy guiding grace afford—teach me thy way!
> Help me to walk aright,
> More by faith, less by sight;
> Lead me with heav'nly light—teach me thy way!
>
> When I am sad at heart, teach me thy way!
> When earthly joys depart, teach me thy way!
> In hours of loneliness,
> In times of dire distress,
> In failure or success, teach me thy way!
>
> When doubts and fears arise, teach me thy way!
> When storms o'erspread the skies, teach me thy way!
> Shine through the cloud and rain,
> Through sorrow, toil and pain;
> Make thou my pathway plain—teach me thy way!
>
> E. Mansell Ramsey

NOTE

[1] The Gallup Organization, *The Unchurched American: 10 Years Later* (Princeton: Princeton Religious Research Center, 1988) 2–4.

10

THE CHRISTIAN ASSEMBLY

Hebrews 10:19–25

Ned had not been to his class meeting or preaching in several months. Life had been rough since his wife had died in the spring. He found himself apathetic where he had once felt enthusiastic, and his absence from his beloved Methodist society revealed his depression.[1]

The class leader had contacted him often, and stopped to talk with him whenever they met on the street. One day he came to call. Ned's home was a humble cottage on the edge of a village below the moors of the West Riding of Yorkshire. The day was cool and the class leader found Ned sitting beside a warm fire, now burned down to blue-tinged flames on shimmering embers. The class leader entered at Ned's beckoning, and without more than a word of greeting took another chair before the fire. In silence the two men gazed at the blaze, the dancing flames rising from irridescent coals.

After some minutes in the quietness, the class leader picked up a poker and maneuvered a glowing coal out of the fire and onto the hearth. As the two men watched, the ember darkened, cooled, grew grey and cold. Without another word, the class leader thumped Ned on the shoulder and took his leave. Ned understood, far better than we, the meaning of the strange, silent parable. He decided then and there that he would be in class and chapel the next week.

Early Methodists believed in church attendance. In fact, three months' voluntary absence from class meeting usually meant removal from the society's membership roll. But church attendance was not a ritual nor mere habit for them. It was life. Without that regular contact with fellow believers, the Methodists feared that zeal and concern would fade. But things are different today. One-third of my church's members are never in church, and too many others come sporadically. Need I say that I am concerned about the cooling of isolated embers?

In an almost off-hand comment, our Hebrew brother first calls attention to the theme of Christian fellowship that figures so prominently in later chapters. At this point I shall limit myself to the one basic question: "Why must Christians meet together?"

Getting Christians to attend the assembly regularly has been a problem almost from the beginning of the church. Within a generation of the time Paul (then Saul) mounted his donkey and headed for Damascus in pursuit of fleeing believers, the writer of the epistle to the Hebrews was already painfully aware of many who were neglecting the assembly. He exhorted: "Let us consider how we may spur one another on toward love and good deeds. Let us not give up meeting together, as some are in the habit of doing, but let us encourage one another—and all the more as you see the Day approaching" (10:25).

Those early Christians did not have all the problems about traditions, preaching styles, hermeneutical approaches, choirs, soloists, robes, and thermostats. Yet there were already some who habitually neglected the assembly.

I have been confronted many times by a recalcitrant church member who argues, "But I don't have to go to church to be a Christian." It seems, too, that such opinions form a national consensus. The Gallup Poll referred to above shows that seventy-six percent of all Americans believe that a person can be a faithful Christian without attending church.[2] I used to find it frustrating that nowhere in the New Testament, except in this passage, is attendance at the assembly commanded. There is, however, ample evidence to suggest that the biblical writers assumed that believers would be there. There is no question about the habits of Jesus himself: "On the Sabbath day he went into the synagogue, as was his custom" (Luke 4:16). Paul made a point of attending at every opportunity (Acts 9:20; 13:5, 14). He certainly expected the Corinthians to be in the assembly on the first day of the week (1 Cor. 16:2).

More evidence comes for the terms that biblical writers use to describe the church. Every one of them (even *church* itself) communicates a collective image: the body of Christ, the bride of Christ, the temple of God, the priesthood, the people of God. We look in vain for any statement that dissociates the child of God from the family of God. Christians belong together, they "are all members of one body" (Eph. 4:25). But there has always been a problem in relating the universal church as a theological tenet to the local congregation that meets in a building at Fifth and Main.

The medieval church taught that salvation was impossible apart from the visible church and its sacraments (so folks had to come at least once in a while). That approach didn't result in faithful attendance. Neither did laws requiring church attendance. The Reformers also tried to force attendance but soon gave it up. In fact, the Protestant Reformation denied any link whatsoever between salvation and good works, and church attendance was simply another good work.

We Americans have compounded the problem by concentrating almost exclusively on the believer's relationship with God to the neglect of the relationship with other believers. How many books on the moral necessity of the church have you read? And how many evangelists teach the Five Spiritual Laws? (Five? That's right. The Fifth Law is that true faith will motivate a believer to seek out the fellowship of other believers.) Attendance at a Bible-believing church is recommended in a closing paragraph entitled "The Importance of a Good Church." It is a true statement, but why is it an addendum? What about the fact that a direct relationship exists between true saving faith and Christian fellowship?

I may sound heretical. But there is more than a grain of truth to the position of the medieval church. No person will ever be eternally saved without becoming a part of the church of Jesus Christ. This is true of the spiritual body of Christ, but it is also conditionally true of the local congregation. The visible congregation is the tangible expression of the spiritual church.

The Reformers almost lost that kernel of truth in defending salvation by faith alone. Perhaps not until the Evangelical Awakening of the eighteenth century—the Methodist movement in particular—was it fully recovered, only to be almost lost again. The truth is this: *No Christian can be responsive to God and at the same time neglect or shun the regular assembly of Christians.*

I know, of course, that a staggering distance separates the ideal world of theology and the real world of local congregations. I know that typical American worship services are a far cry from the spontaneous and interactive meetings of early Christians. Many "worship" services are devoid of fellowship (with either God or believers).

Obviously, our brother writing here did not have in mind the impersonal services of suburban American congregations. If the preaching I sometimes hear on my local Christian radio station is representative of the preaching in my county, horrors! If the reception I receive when I attend an ecumenical Thanksgiving Service is indicative of the warmth and fellowship in our local congregations, heaven help us!

I can tell story after story about emotional ambushes that have been mounted against vulnerable people in the name of Christ. And I suppose every person who has ever been a part of a congregation has been deeply injured at some point by thoughtless or selfish church people—many have been mutilated. Regardless of how defective they may be, our services, Sunday school classes, and Bible studies are Christian assemblies.

I have heard all the excuses: the uninspiring preaching, the unfriendly people, the unpleasant experiences. Yes, and the church has—and always will have—more than its share of hypocrites and snobs. But put all the negatives in one basket, and its weight will hardly register against one biblical fact: the Christian assembly is a necessity. Believers must find a

Christian fellowship if they are to be responsive to the grace of God.

The best explanation is again an analogy. Many Christians think of the church as a giant institutional machine that functions more or less independently of its individual parts. Individuals plug into or pull out of the machine as they choose without serious loss either to themselves or to the machine. But the primary biblical analogies are of either a body or a family. And either analogy calls to mind a web of relationships. God's church is an intricate web of many strands, each strand a personal relationship.

Think of the strands of relationship that exist between you and the members of your Sunday school class, your Bible study group, and your church. A complex web, isn't it? Add to that web the equally complex web of relationships between pastor and people. Wrap all of those in another web because each individual is personally linked with the resident Savior. Then look beyond those webs to the strands that join believers with nonbelieving neighbors outside the fellowship. It may at times appear hopelessly tangled or frustratingly disorganized. But in fact the church is lovingly crafted and energized strand by strand by the indwelling Holy Spirit. Awesome!

LOVE CREATES RELATIONSHIPS

It was pure love in the beginning that motivated God to create a family of human beings who had independent wills. I remember a poster that years ago made a great impression on me. It was a picture of a hand outstretched, releasing a bird to take its flight. The caption read something like this: "If you truly love someone, let him go. If he returns to you, he is really yours. If he does not, he was never yours to begin with." God certainly understood the risk he took, for he foresaw the rebellion of his creatures. But he could not truly love without granting true freedom.

Yet an independent will did not make Adam independent. Even before the Fall he needed Eve. Never in all the fallen world since has any person been whole or complete if isolated from loving relationships with companions. God uses this primal cry for intimate relationship to redeem us from the curse of sin. It is in the loving fellowship of God's church that we experience the love of God. It is there that we find ourselves serving as channels of God's love to others. Enmeshed in the Spirit-energized web of God's church we love and are loved.

RELATIONSHIPS MOLD CHARACTER

Remember the old gem of common wisdom that says, "Birds of a feather flock together"? To put that in other words, "Show me a person's friends, and I will tell you that person's character." The writer of this epistle has already taught us that Jesus is sanctifying us. We are being conformed to his image day by day, year by year. We are at times unaware of the extent to which our companions mold our character. But we are being molded.

The believer who isolates himself from the fellowship of the church by neglect or choice chooses to be molded by nonbelievers. What quicker way is there to deface the sanctifying work of God? But in the mesh of the church, we voluntarily expose ourselves to the washing, cleansing work of God in our lives through our brothers and sisters. To refuse that association is to choose, by default, conformity with our fallen society.

CHARACTER DETERMINES VALUES

One of the challenging themes of the Bible is that Christians are strangers and pilgrims in this world. We do not belong here; this is not our home. The Christian is a citizen of another world in addition to his human citizenship here. The values of that other world are in conflict with the values of this world. Sometimes that conflict is violent, sometimes it is muted, but it is unending.

It is in the Christian assembly that Christians can shake off the barnacles of earthly values, which adhere to us so easily. The slow and painful process of reorganizing our priorities simply.will not happen if we avoid the challenges of Christian fellowship. Not everyone in the fellowship is truly Christian, for Jesus told us that weeds are there as well. But God's people are here; every growing believer is a part of some fellowship.

FELLOWSHIP EXPANDS KNOWLEDGE

If we are citizens of heaven while living here on earth, then we are going to have real problems because we have never been in heaven. We have no experience with that world, no firsthand knowledge of its laws or its privileges. We cannot rely on our own experience. We must then find guidance and direction from God himself.

He could have, I suppose, designed a plan in which he had nothing but direct, personal contact with his followers, one by one. But he didn't. Rather, he created the church and gave to that church the responsibility to proclaim and embody his Word. No doubt the ministry of Christian radio and television can do much to teach Christian values and biblical insights, but the ministry of the Word of God is more than intellectual content. It is personal training and discipline, and that can never be found in front of the TV. It must be learned in interaction with other Christians.

COMPANIONSHIP OVERCOMES WEAKNESS

Someone once said, "A person who is accountable to no one can never reach more than sixty percent of his potential." That is probably an overstatement. Our native laziness militates against our not-so-constant desire to swim upstream spiritually. Our inexperience in the world of the spiritual has the same impact on us. In the assembly we find the motivation that we call "Christian discipline." Though discipline is lax in our churches, it is not completely extinguished. Encouragement is a form of discipline, and so is the sharing of goals, the shouldering of responsibility, and the give and take of fellowship. All of this is the sanctifying discipline of God, given to us through fellow believers.

If we cut ourselves off from his discipline, we are but

illegitimate children (Heb. 12:8). If our eternal salvation comes to us through our relationship with Jesus Christ, as Christ taught in the parable of the vine (John 15:1–6), then we must take seriously the form in which God has chosen to relate to us. He has created a church composed of those who believe. The fundamental purpose of the church is to provide for us the spiritual climate in which our response to God can take hold, hang on, and grow.

The Christian assembly stimulates us to prepare for the interrelatedness and interdependence of heaven. No Christian can be responsive to God and at the same time neglect or shun the regular assembly of Christians. So "let us consider how we may spur one another on toward love and good deeds. Let us not give up meeting together, as some are in the habit of doing, but let us encourage one another—and all the more as you see the Day approaching."

> All praise to our redeeming Lord,
> Who joins us by his grace,
> And binds us, each to each restored,
> Together seek his face.
>
> He bids us build each other up;
> And, gathered into one,
> To our high calling's glorious hope,
> We hand in hand go on.
>
> The gift which he on one bestows,
> We all delight to prove;
> The grace through every vessel flows,
> In purest streams of love.
>
> We all partake the joy of one,
> The common peace we feel:
> A peace to sensual minds unknown,
> A joy unspeakable.
>
> Charles Wesley

NOTES

[1] This chapter appeared originally in *Good News* 23, no. 2 (September/October 1989): 23–25. Used by permission.

[2] *Unchurched American,* 3.

11

THE UNEXPECTED TREASURES OF COMPANIONSHIP

Hebrews 10:32–39

John Wesley recorded in his Journal for March 5, 1738:

> I found my brother at Oxford, recovering from his pleurisy; and with him Peter Böhler; by whom (in the hand of the great God) I was, on Sunday, the 5th, clearly convinced of unbelief, of the want of that faith whereby alone we are saved. Immediately it struck into my mind, "Leave off preaching. How can you preach to others, who have not faith yourself?" I asked Böhler, whether he thought I should leave it off or not. He answered, "By no means . . . Preach faith till you have it; and then because you have it, you will preach faith."[1]

At no time am I more painfully conscious of being a product of twentieth-century American evangelicalism than I am when I confront a strange phrase like that in Hebrews 10:34: "joyfully accepting the confiscation of your property." How can two totally different and contradictory ideas like "joy" and "confiscation" occur in the same sentence? Yet that phrase described the early Hebrew Christian church.

But could it ever describe me? I certainly identify with Wesley's sentiments. Should I even try to write about an area of my own life that is so far short? I, too, will take Peter Böhler's advice, and continue to write until I have the joyful disdain for material possessions that marked these ancient Christians, as our Hebrew pastor described them in 10:32–39.

The Hebrew church was at grave risk of turning her back on Jesus as Savior. We evangelicals face another risk of equal concern. Where their danger lay in the tightening grip of legalism, we are being strangled by materialism. We instinctively want to believe that what glorifies God and is good for his kingdom is always materially good for us. It seems incomprehensible and offensive to us that our God of love could be glorified more by our suffering or loss than by our prosperity.

I was a student at Asbury College when God visited the campus and community with spontaneous revival in 1970. That movement of the Spirit spread in subsequent weeks to dozens of college campuses and churches all across the nation. I have experienced revival, and I long to see God send revival throughout the country. I see no other way out of the moral morass into which we have fallen. I hear the prayer for revival rising from the lips of countless other Christians as well.

But—and that is a very big *but*—if history offers any reliable insight for us, it is this: prosperous people tend not to pray. Perhaps our earnest prayers for revival can be answered only in a catastrophic collapse of our Western economy. If the price of revival is material loss, who is willing to pay? In my wildest nightmares I cannot imagine the spiritual and emotional chaos that would come to our "Bible-believing" churches if we were suddenly stripped of our hefty incomes and cozy homes and elegant wardrobes. How many would turn their backs on God because he had "failed" them?

It is time, I am convinced, for us to take a long hard look at the terms of our companionship with our God. Our Hebrew writer made one central point again and again: God established the terms of our relationship with him. We only respond; we never dictate. But when we respond to his invitation, we discover some of the most amazing benefits and in the strangest circumstances. Horace Walpole coined the term *serendipity* to describe the main characters in the tale *The Three Princes of Serendip*. Serendipity is an aptitude for making fortunate discoveries accidentally, of finding treasures in unlikely places.

Our Hebrews author uses four phrases to describe the early Hebrew Christian believers, and each of them is a kind of serendipity. Not one of these statements is initially attractive, but each contains an amazing benefit that cannot be discovered until the difficulties swarm over us. Ready for the plunge?

ENDURING PERSECUTION

"Sometimes you were publicly exposed to insult and persecution" (10:33). The Hebrew church is the church of the early chapters of Acts. These Christians had endured a great deal. It had not been easy to be a Christian. The persecution first broke out with the stoning of Stephen. With his death, everything caved in on this new and inexperienced Christian fellowship. One of the leaders had been martyred, and the authorities hounded the trails of other Christians.

Believers were forced to scatter over the Judean country-side and even into Samaria and Galilee and on to Syria. But even though they were suffering for their faith, they were preaching the Gospel as they went. Running for their lives, stripped of their possessions, they eagerly told everyone they met, "I have good news for you!" "Absurd!" we moderns might say. "Good news my foot! What about all God's promises of prosperity and good health?" If we were forced out of our homes, stripped of our property, and left to wander, could we go joyfully, preaching the Gospel of Christ?

Persecution intensified. Saul hunted believers everywhere, throwing them into prison and, probably, confiscating their property in the name of the Sanhedrin. By the time this epistle was written, these believers had felt the heavy hand of the empire as well. The emperor had issued a decree banishing all Christians and Jews from Rome. This was the first step in a tightening web of persecution that was to cost thousands of Christians their lives. Yet they had endured up to this point.

Endurance is a mark of a true Christian: the ability to hang on when things are at their worst. One of the proofs of the resurrection of Jesus Christ is the fact that his disciples were later willing to give their lives for the truth of the Resurrection.

If this had been an elaborate hoax to deceive the authorities, or if the disciples were in this new movement for personal gain, do you believe that they would have died rather than forsake the name of Christ?

No! People don't die for things they don't believe in. They were convinced. Jesus Christ was real and alive! If that was true, then there was nothing else on the face of the earth that really mattered except his approval. What is there about the approval of God that causes Christians to endure persecution? What value do we find that causes us to accept, and even ignore, the disdain of others? David understood. He wrote, "Surely you have granted [the king himself] eternal blessings and made him glad with the joy of your presence" (Ps. 21:6).

I don't intend to confuse joy with happiness. Happiness is a superficial emotional state, and joy is a deep, quiet calm of the innermost being. Joy is never found by looking for it. It is only a by-product of the presence of God. We experience his presence only as we learn to depend on him completely. And apart from necessity, little persuades us to depend on God. Isn't it strange that our human search for happiness leads us to avoid the painful and trying times? We can spend our lives avoiding the path to joy and miss the treasure we seek.

TAKING SIDES WITH THE OPPRESSED

"At other times you stood side by side with those who were so treated." (10:33). God built into our psychological makeup a drive to preserve our own lives. When we are threatened, we will fight for life. To every attack, physical or verbal, our first impulse is to defend ourselves. But here was a Christian fellowship where the first impulse was, "We must be with our brothers and sisters who are suffering."

There was no consideration of personal safety, comfort, or reputation. You couldn't keep these people apart! When a brother or sister was suffering, it didn't matter what it cost. These were bonds that could not be broken by threats to personal well-being. And this is the church of Jesus at its best.

What kind of bonds were these that not only bound these believers to God, but to each other?

The greatest deception in our world today is the pervasive notion that we will find the reason for our lives within ourselves. We pass this way only once; get all we can out of life because we won't have another chance. We must be true to ourselves first. This is the path to happiness, we are taught, and as a nation we are on a binge of self-gratification. We want and we want, and we want more and more of it.

Self-denial is a dirty word. It is an out-of-date concept. Nobody denies himself anything anymore. The whole point of American life is to get everything we can get. But here were Christians who would risk everything, including life itself, to stand beside a brother or sister under persecution. The fact that comforting a friend who was being persecuted might cost one his own property simply had no weight. No price was too high to be a part of the church of Jesus Christ. These people knew how to love; they stuck together.

Selflessness that allows us to bury ourselves in the suffering of brothers and sisters is a mark of true Christian faith. Jesus himself said, "Whoever finds his life will lose it, and whoever loses his life for my sake will find it" (Matt. 10:39). And this selflessness is precisely what Jesus was referring to when he told his disciples, "By this all men will know that you are my disciples, if you love one another" (John 13:35). To our modern ears, isn't this a strange recipe for joy?

We find joy in the presence of God, but we want to avoid the suffering that opens the path into his presence. And we find joy in our relationship with God's people, though we are sorely tempted at times to keep to ourselves. But as long as personal preferences and material possessions are more important than our relationships with fellow Christians, we are condemned by our own selfishness to a joyless existence. The two supreme treasures on earth are our bonds with fellow Christians and our bond with Christ. Both are forged in the fires of affliction, and both give us the joy we crave.

LOVING FOR THE LONG HAUL

"You sympathized with those in prison" (10:34). Prisons today are not pleasant places, but they were infinitely worse in the first century—filthy, dark, unheated, and without sanitary facilities. Men and women were thrown into them and usually forgotten. In those wretched places crawling with vermin they died. The government did not provide three square meals a day. It didn't provide anything. No shelter, no blankets, no food; nothing but a guard.

If a prisoner were to survive, he had to be cared for by members of his family or his friends. Prisons were used to house offenders until trial or punishment, but length of stay was uncertain. Providing daily necessities of life for a prisoner was a tedious and dangerous business. Those who came to visit exposed themselves to the worst kinds of conditions.

Perhaps sympathy for prisoners was the ultimate expression of compassion. Yet even in such extreme conditions, loyalty to the brother or sister in prison reflected the presence of God. He is not put off by suffering, danger, or disgrace. Even more, there is no time limit on his compassion; he never reaches burnout.

We Christians do react in love when a crisis occurs in our circle of friends. Our offer of help is usually structured and guided by social custom, and beyond those customary guidelines we hesitate to go. But the loyalty that is the mark of true Christians goes far beyond that. It takes something extraordinary to care through years of illness or suffering—or years of imprisonment. How often the chronically ill are shunned or shut up because there seems to be no end to the demands they place on their companions.

If joy is born in companionship with God and his children, then it comes as no surprise that we discover joy through loyalty. Jesus explained that in meeting the needs of others, we are in fact doing personal service to him. Beyond the physical exhaustion, emotional drain, and unending demands, there is joy. For we find his presence when we serve him.

BREAKING THE POWER OF
MATERIAL POSSESSIONS

That brings us to this fascinating phrase "joyfully accepting the confiscation of your property" (10:34). We don't take the loss of material possessions very gracefully. I confess to being one of the original tightwads in this world. I remember several years ago losing a ten-dollar bill. I don't remember the details, but I do remember the pain! I searched through my pockets and my car; I mentally retraced my day place by place again and again. The frustration and anger lasted for several days. I put myself through agony. I was angry with myself and everyone close to me. All over a ten-dollar bill!

Neither do I accept gracefully being hoodwinked. And since I am a soft touch for anyone in trouble with a good story, I get taken all too often. The feelings are the same: it hurts terribly to be the butt of injustice. I suspect that most Americans must feel the same way because we have succeeded in jamming our court dockets to the breaking point as we seek redress for wrongs done to us.

Yet here I come face to face with a body of Christians who could be described as accepting joyfully the confiscation of their property. What is wrong with these people? Such injustice! I'm sure that they felt pain also. These Christians were as human as we are. It hurt. But that is not the end of the phrase. The writer continues, ". . . because you knew that you yourselves had better and lasting possessions." Perhaps these early Christians knew something about God that we do not really believe.

Much of our time is consumed in preparing for the future, and that in itself is no problem. Wise stewardship of our resources requires that we plan as best we can. God is pleased with that care. But in the attitude behind the planning and preparation we find our trouble. Down deep we fear that in the crises that experience teaches us to expect, we will be caught short. "What if . . . " lies at the heart of the insurance agent's sales pitch, and it has a barb that fastens itself deep in the soul. Our deepest motivation is to protect ourselves in the unknown and unknowable future.

With all our skill, money, and opportunity, we cannot protect ourselves from the future. Neither can we ever fully escape a sense of defenselessness when we think of the years ahead. What if there is another market crash? What if we experience another devastating depression? What if we become seriously or chronically ill? The fear runs deep and turbulently beneath our consciousness, unsettling our rest and robbing us of joy. What an awful reality to be powerless in an overpowering world where others make choices that may rip from us all our defenses and all our provisions in a moment of time.

The Hebrew Christians had accepted a truth about God that we do not: God is sufficient. If he is in fact all-powerful, he can take care of every conceivable and inconceivable threat to me. If God is love, he will take care of me, ungrudgingly. If God can and will meet every threat, it is only common sense to turn over all my affairs and all my anxiety to him.

What about this Companion who wishes to walk with me through the valleys and over the mountains of my life? I know about him. But why am I so reluctant to trust him? These Hebrew Christians had been convinced that for every item they lost, their Companion would grant to them something of greater worth. Nor did they anticipate those greater possessions merely in material terms. Few of them ever had anything, and many ended their lives at the wrong end of the executioner's sword. But those greater possessions remained. They possessed the peace of God and the love of a fellowship of brothers and sisters that no earthly power could destroy.

And there is joy. In breaking our dependence on all forms of earthly security, by taking from us the very things we are sure we need, God leads us to joy. How much better, how much wiser and more reasonable, it would be for us to lay our defenses in our Father's hands, to resign our future into God's control. Once we experience the joy of companionship with God, we will never want to settle for anything less. We will be amazed at our stupidity for hesitating so long. We will look at the feeble securities of this world, and wonder with amazement that we could ever have depended on them.

As I confessed at the beginning, I have not yet arrived at

the joyful relationship I see in the distance. I am learning to trust God, yet still at times grudgingly and with many backward glances. But already I have found a measure of joy that I have not found anywhere else. That taste whets my appetite for more. I turn to face and accept the suffering and misfortune that is my lot in this cursed world. I am not a fatalist or a masochist, and I find no pleasure or attraction in suffering. But I walk with God. His companionship is worth it all, ten thousand times over.

> In heavenly love abiding,
> No change my heart shall fear;
> And safe is such confiding,
> For nothing changes here.
> The storm may roar without me,
> My heart may low be laid;
> But God is round about me,
> And can I be dismayed?
>
> Wherever he may guide me,
> No want shall turn me back;
> My Shepherd is beside me,
> And nothing can I lack.
> His wisdom ever waketh,
> His sight is never dim;
> He knows the way he taketh,
> And I will walk with him.
>
> Green pastures are before me,
> Which yet I have not seen;
> Bright skies will soon be o'er me,
> Where darkest clouds have been.
> My hope I cannot measure,
> My path to life is free;
> My Savior has my treasure,
> And he will walk with me.
>   Anna Laetitia Waring

NOTE

[1] *Journals and Diaries I*, eds. W. Reginald Ward and Richard P. Heitzenrater, vol. 18 of *The Works of John Wesley* (Nashville: Abingdon, 1988), 228.

12

FAITH, RESPONSE, AND ACTION

Hebrews 11:1–31

My younger son Philip was anticipating his eleventh birthday. A day or two earlier he had received a birthday card from his grandmother. A birthday card from grandmother usually included a check. He was noticeably disappointed when he opened the card and found nothing. Then he found a note at the bottom of the card. "Philip, I have your birthday present, and I will send it home with your mother next week." His face brightened, and all trace of disappointment vanished. That was all it took; things were fine.

My wife and I were at grandmother's the following week while our sons stayed with friends. Usually it seems that they hardly miss us, but this time Philip telephoned us several times. He wanted to know exactly when we were coming home. He didn't want to know the day (he already knew that); he wanted the hour and the minute. He never said it aloud, but he knew that I knew that in the back of his mind was the promise of that birthday present. The problem was not *whether* the present was coming; it was *when* it was to arrive. He could hardly wait until he held it in his hands, but he was already convinced of the reality of the gift.

The source of Philip's certainty was his grandmother's word in black and white: "I will send your birthday present with your mother next week." If he had thought it out, he might have followed steps like these:

A. This is my grandmother's promise.
B. She has always proved reliable before, and has always done what she said she would do.
C. Therefore, I believe she is telling the truth this time also.
D. I might be setting myself up for disappointment, but I will take that risk.
E. Therefore, I accept the reality of her gift, though I have not yet seen it.

Faith is our response to the gracious promise of God. Such faith is the heart of our relationship with God. The familiar cadences of Hebrews 11 ring with the themes of grace and response—and always in that order. If we are to walk as companions of God through a world like this, we must have one thing clear and settled. In this relationship of grace, all the initiative comes from God. Our highest ambitions can only reflect his intentions. Our most fervent and effective prayers are nothing more than echoes of his spoken word. Even our best work is only the fruit of his love. Therefore, true faith has no agenda of its own. It is a reflection of the will of God.

FAITH IS RESPONSE

I hear almost every week a fellow Christian say, "If I only had enough faith, God would . . . heal me (or my friend) . . . provide a new car for me . . . give me that promotion I have been working for . . . change my spouse's attitude . . . save my wandering son. . . ." That attitude shows up on plaques such as "Prayer Changes Things." We would like to believe that we can force God to do what we want him to do by putting on the pressure, i.e., praying hard and long. The mental picture I form is someone with clenched fists and jaw, face screwed up with an expression of intense effort, working to believe.

But Philip didn't work at all to believe that his grandmother was going to send his birthday present. His was a calm (as opposed to *worried*) anticipation of what was going to happen. He did not believe that the gift would materialize because he worked at visualizing it. He had no part in the offer of the gift; his was an eager response to the offer of another. He had his grandmother's word, and he believed her.

In the conservative "old-fashioned" churches where I grew up, Christians talked about "praying through." It has taken me years to understand what they were talking about. As I heard that phrase over and over (sometimes it was only a cliché), I formed the impression that when you had "prayed through" you had prayed so long and so hard that you had forced God to do what he would not have done otherwise; you had changed his mind. But even as a young Christian, I had a nagging suspicion that God was not going to do what I wanted him to do regardless of my most intense prayers.

I have learned that I (and a host of fellow Christians) had actually reversed the order. I had been initiating action and expecting God to respond to my initiative. But since we can initiate nothing of value, prayer and faith are my responses to God's initiative—his grace. Before I can believe, I must have something to believe. Once I hear the promise of God, then I can respond. But not before.

This is "praying through." The old saints had prayed until they had heard God speak! They had prayed until they sorted through the clamoring of their own desires and the babble of others' expectations, and had recognized the authentic voice of God. Once they heard him speak, they could respond.

Paul Cho tells a story that helped clarify for me the responsive character of true faith. Three young Korean Christian girls were traveling to a youth campaign on Samgak Mountain. The three were part of a large group stranded on the wrong side of a rain-swollen river. The girls decided that since by faith Peter had walked on water, they could by faith wade through the flood. So they prayed, quoted Bible verses, and waded in. All three were swept away to their deaths.

The impact was staggering: even national newspapers picked up the story. The girls were apparently practicing what they had been taught: that God would protect and prosper anyone who stepped out in faith and obedience. It seemed that God had failed to honor the sincere faith of these young people.

Cho himself was shaken and he turned to the Scriptures. God showed him, after an extended and painful time of study, that the girls had acted on a general knowledge of God's Word but that they had not listened for God's specific word for this occasion. They had presumed on God. They initiated the "miracle." They expected God to respond to their decision.[1]

Perhaps many other Christians have lost their lives by demanding a particular response from God. Newspapers have carried stories of suffering and death because "faith healers" told followers to trust God and not seek medical help. But many others are guilt-ridden and spiritually confused because they stepped out "in faith," and God wasn't there to catch them. He didn't follow the script they had handed him.

When we have the word of someone we love and trust, it is not difficult to accept that word and live in expectation of its fulfillment. This is faith. When we hear God's promise, then in faith we respond: "Lord, I understand that you have always been faithful to fulfill your promises. Even though I risk disappointment, I accept your promise as real and anticipate receiving your gift." This and this alone is biblical faith.

So don't rifle through your Bible to find a verse about that new car you want. We are not talking about having our way but about learning God's will. There is nothing impersonal and mechanical about biblical faith. No formulas guarantee answers to prayer. Faith is the by-product of the loving relationship between a child and a parent.

Over a period of years Philip had come to trust his grandmother's word. As she fulfilled each promise, his confidence grew. He had spent time with her and knew her personally. Had the same offer come from a stranger, his response would have been different, more along the lines of "I'll believe it when I see it." But his faith in his grandmother grew naturally out of his relationship with her.

We are not told in this passage that God spoke first to Abel, though other verses imply that God had already instituted animal sacrifice for sin. Neither are we told that Enoch first heard from God. But from that point on, every "by faith" is preceded by a "God said." "By faith Noah, when warned. . . ." "By faith Abraham, when called. . . ." "By faith Abraham . . . was enabled to become a father because he considered him faithful who had made the promise" (v. 11). "By faith Abraham, when God tested him. . . ." (v. 17) Moses must have heard the call of God (v. 24), and certainly the walls of Jericho fell because God spoke first (v. 30).

We would rather act on what we want to believe is God's will than spend the time and humble ourselves to hear what God actually says to us. Our decisive action is applauded as "good leadership." We get on with the business at hand and can list our "accomplishments" in the church record. But we are doomed—at best—to "accomplish" only what can be done by human skill and wisdom alone. At worst, we recklessly endanger the reputation of God and undermine the confidence of those who trust us. No, the time spent in waiting on the word of God is time spent for the sake of eternity.

FAITH IS ACTION

Responsive faith is more than assent; it is movement. Each "by faith" is coupled with action. "By faith Abel offered. . . ." "By faith Noah . . . built an ark." "By faith Abraham . . . obeyed and went. . . ." "By faith Abraham . . . offered Isaac. . . ." "By faith Isaac blessed. . . ." "By faith Jacob blessed. . . ." "By faith Joseph . . . gave instructions." "By faith Moses' parents hid him. . . ." "By faith Moses . . . refused. . . ."

I could list the rest of them, but the pattern is clear. In fact, our Hebrew author compiled this Hall of Faith to make precisely this point. Faith is not merely an intellectual process. It is neither the mastery of facts nor the comprehension of ideas. True faith always results in movement.

Two kinds of active response are described here. First, "Anyone who comes to him must believe that he exists and that he rewards those who earnestly seek him." Through the grace of God we come to know who he is. At that point we choose to respond to his invitation to draw close (that is faith) or we turn and walk away (that is unbelief). Spiritual movement may or may not involve physical action, but it is action nevertheless. For me, that response meant walking forward to kneel at the Communion rail of a college chapel. For you, it might have been pulling off the highway or taking the Gideon Bible from the dresser drawer in a motel room. It might have been a phone call or a whispered prayer. It could be any of ten thousand responses, but each response is action.

Spiritual movement always results in physical movement of some sort. Every one of those verbs that follow "by faith" are action words. *Offered, built, went, blessed, hid, refused, welcomed:* all describe action. Take Noah, for instance. His faith resulted in a century-long building program—a hundred years of physical labor to carry out the commands of an invisible God in the face of the taunts of an entire civilization. He could have professed faith in God every minute of that century, but had he not worked, he would have died. His "faith" would have availed him nothing.

We have made a strategic error in the twentieth century. We have convinced ourselves that all it takes to be a Christian is sincere repetition of a prescribed formula: "Yes, I believe in Jesus Christ, and I accept him as my Savior. I am sorry for my sins, and ask him to forgive me." That may be the first step of faith, but it is not faith. Anyone can say words.

Too many believe that they are Christians because they said some words, but their lives do not demonstrate living faith. Again, we could go through the entire passage and describe characteristics of living faith. I will use just the first three Heroes of Faith as examples.

First, Abel's faith produced acceptable worship. Today worship is almost a lost art! True faith begins when we wait for and hear the word of God to us. The first act of faith is our approach to the Father through Jesus, at his invitation. Yet our churches are filled on Sunday morning with professing Christians who do not hear nor approach God. And I fear that it is we—evangelical leaders and teachers—who have taught them to feel secure in their intellectual acceptance of theological propositions. O God, break our hearts in your presence!

Second, living faith produces hunger for God, as the story of Enoch reveals. Bud Robinson said he believed that Enoch and God went out for a walk one evening. They walked on and on, deeply absorbed in their fellowship. When they finally realized how long they had spent together and how far they had walked, God turned to Enoch and said, "Enoch, we are closer to my house than yours. Why don't you come home with me and spend the night?" But Enoch was not the only example. Abraham was God's friend; Moses pleaded to see God's glory. David's heart sought after God, and Jeremiah's tears reflected the weeping heart of God. Jesus said, "Blessed are those who hunger and thirst for righteousness, for they shall be filled" (Matt. 5:6). True faith is reflected in spiritual hunger.

Third, living faith produces obedience. Noah must be the world's least effective evangelist. After a century of preaching he counted only seven converts—the members of his own family. His faith expressed itself in such a radical obedience that he stood alone against an entire civilization. By its definition, faith is taking the Word of God at face value. If God said it, Noah believed it, and then reorganized his whole life around it. All he needed to know was what God said. Everything else revolved around that Word.

If we are to experience the power of God in our day, it will begin when we shift our sights from the gifts of God to God himself. We are called to follow his agenda and to respond to his initiatives.

> My God and Father, while I stray
> Far from my home in life's rough way,
> O teach me from my heart to say,
> "Thy will be done."
>
> If thou shouldst call me to resign
> What I most prize, if ne'er was mine.
> I only yield thee what was thine:
> Thy will be done.
>
> Let but my fainting heart be blest
> With thy sweet Spirit for its quest;

My God, to thee I leave the rest:
Thy will be done.

Renew my will from day to day;
Blend it with thine; and take away
All that now makes it hard to say,
Thy will be done.

Charlotte Elliott

NOTE

[1] Paul Yonggi Cho, *The Fourth Dimension* (South Plainfield, N.J.: Bridge Publishing, 1979), 91–93.

13

WHEN CHRISTIANS SUFFER

Hebrews 11:32–40
Hebrews 12:4–11

I am a white American. I have never struggled with discrimination or hatred because of my color. I am also male so I have not felt the pain of cultural stereotypes faced by Christian women. I was born in a nation where tolerance is a virtue, and I have not been persecuted for my faith. I am healthy and so is my family. I have never experienced the agony of chronic pain nor wrestled with physical or mental handicaps. My parents are living and in good health. I have not carried the exhausting burden of a helpless loved one. Nor have I suffered the death of someone dear.

I have, however, fought long difficult battles—some of which I have already shared in the pages of this book. But the battles I have faced seem so different, so much less terrible, than the battles some of my friends and companions face. I am grateful. But I am also reluctant to write this chapter. If I should rewrite this chapter twenty years from now, it would ring with a far deeper resonance than it does now. May God grant me the courage, until then, to live by the principles I explore.

Imagine yourself standing on the fifty-yard line at the center of the field at the Rose Bowl. The stadium is sold out. The cheering is uncomfortably loud, even at this distance from the stands. Allow your mental picture to expand: that stadium becomes a hundred times larger. It is filled, not with football fanatics, but with throngs of white-robed saints from all the ages of human history. They, too, are cheering: swelling a thundering chorus of praise to God who sits on his throne.

As you survey the happy multitude, you understand somehow that two groups are in the stadium. On one side are those who experienced remarkable victories here on earth. Our Hebrew author lists a few of them: Abel, Enoch, Noah, Abraham, Isaac, Jacob, Joseph, Moses, Rahab, Gideon, Barak, Samson, Jephthah, David, and Samuel. They are joined by thousands of others who have seen God transform impossible circumstances to the wonder and amazement of the world.

On the other side of the stadium is another crowd, probably much larger than the first one. They too, are praising God for his power and goodness to them. But their stories are tragic. They were tortured, beaten, ridiculed, and ostracized. In the struggle between right and wrong, between light and darkness, they lost their lives at the hands of their enemies. Everything had caved in, and in apparent defeat they had died.

No one in this group is mentioned by name, but we know some of them from Scripture and history. Isaiah, Jeremiah, James, Peter, and Paul are there. In fact, all of the apostles except John are in that group. Hundreds of Christians died in the Roman Colosseum at the paws and jaws of lions and the hands of gladiators. Today this group continues to swell, for more Christians have died for their faith in the twentieth century than in all the previous history of the church.

In this great cloud of witnesses, which our author describes in chapter 11, two different kinds of people are lumped together: the winners and the losers. That is, some who won and others who lost, by our earthly standards of measure. Yet they all stand shoulder to shoulder in the presence of God. Why did some suffer so much more than others? No question comes closer to the heart of our faith than this one, and God gives us some insight though perhaps not all the detail we would want.

SUFFERING IS NATURAL IN A CURSED WORLD

First, we must face one basic fact: all suffering grows out of the curse that Adam brought upon the whole creation by his sin. His rebellion has brought pain and death into the whole creation, man and animal alike. Every man, woman, and child falls under the curse, and all live in a cursed world. Suffering comes to all of us, Christian and non-Christians alike. Suffering is part of this world, and we are going to suffer as long as we live here. That is not pleasant. But it is the way it is, and we are not going to change it.

And neither is God—not yet. The sooner we make up our minds that God is not going to give us an easy, problem-free, pain-free life, the happier we are going to be and the less grumbling and criticizing we will do. This is life. This is what it is like to live in a world that is cursed by sin. We would suffer if God had nothing at all to do with his world. Pain is a part of this world order. Suffering is normal. If things are going well for you, and you don't have any problems, be patient. Your turn will come.

GOD DOES NOT SEND SUFFERING

Some are tempted to believe that suffering comes because God is punishing us for sin that we have committed. I have had dear Christian saints ask me in tears, "What have I done that God would send this?" And I am glad I can answer, "God didn't send this."

If the Bible reveals anything at all about God, it is this: God's judgment is absolutely fair and just. But we don't have to look far before we discover gross injustice in the distribution of suffering. Someone who lives like the devil apparently escapes without much suffering. Saints of God who walk with him in sweet submission still suffer agony. The God I serve does not treat his children unjustly. The physical, mental, and emotional traumas of life are not punishment from God.

However, we can bring suffering upon ourselves. Consequences are attached to every choice we make. The individual who chooses to disobey God and flaunt God's law will reap the consequences. A young person may disobey God and marry one who is not a dedicated believer. Then down the road his or her life is filled with heartache, disappointment, divorce, and wayward children. But this suffering is the consequence of a choice. And God, out of respect for our independent wills, does not necessarily intercept those consequences. We suffer the effects of the law of sowing and reaping, but not direct punishment from God.

An equally disheartening error is the idea that those who suffer don't have enough faith to be victorious. Look around those grandstands. Was the faith of those who lost weaker than the faith of those who won? How often I have heard this advice given to a suffering Christian: "You must believe God. Claim your deliverance by faith." These misguided souls believe that if we have enough faith, God will heal us, give us better jobs, or silence our tormentors. He'll make life easier for us.

We are haunted by the insidious idea that faith is a way to get God to do what we want him to do. I'm sorry but that's wrong. God does not do what anybody wants him to do. God does what he wills to do. It is his sovereign will that governs our world. Faith is my confident response to his revealed will, and my loving response to his extended hand of grace. Faith is not a form of heavenly currency with which we can purchase comfort. Too many of us have bought the idea that God's chief work is to make his children comfortable. But God is not in the business of making anyone comfortable—at least not on this side of heaven.

GOD SETS LIMITS ON SUFFERING

What does God do then? How is he involved? In the first place, God sets limits on the suffering that comes to us. Paul penned a special promise to those who are tempted, and it applies to all kinds of suffering. "No temptation has seized you except what is common to man. And God is faithful; he will not let you be tempted beyond what you can bear. But when you are tempted, he will also provide a way out so that you can stand up under it" (1 Cor. 10:13).

Those three sentences ought to be memorized by every believer. He is an omniscient God, and he knows everything about us: strengths, weaknesses, qualities, and faults. He is standing guard to see that nothing comes upon us that will destroy us. When some difficulty comes that threatens to crush the life out of us, we have solid confidence: nothing comes to the children of God that can ultimately destroy them.

Our confidence in God's power to limit suffering is bolstered by firsthand testimony: the story of Job. God called attention to Job's obedience, and Satan responded, "You have protected Job and given him everything anyone could want. Of course he serves you. But you let me have him for a few minutes, and he will curse you to your face." God set the limits. "You may touch his possessions, but you cannot lay a finger on him personally." Satan took his wealth, his family, and the support of his wife. Job was able to stand; God had drawn the limits at the right place.

Later, in another exchange, God moved the limits. "Satan, you may afflict his body, but you cannot take his life." Still, Job stood. Had God allowed physical suffering at the beginning on top of sorrow, Job might have been crushed. But God drew the line at the right place at the right time. Satan could not cross those boundaries, and he cannot cross those God draws in our lives. In fact, God takes what Satan designs for our destruction, and sanctifies the suffering so that it actually works to fit us for the presence of God!

There is a second sense in which God limits the suffering we endure. He always brings it to an end. For Job, the trial and suffering ended with a full and complete restoration, plus a far deeper appreciation for the character of God than he had ever had before. But the limits are not always so obvious from our earthly point of view.

Glance around those heavenly grandstands once more. All trace of suffering has been erased, and every tear has been dried. For some, God drew the line in this life. For others, he drew the line at death. But he did draw the line! I know that this seems small comfort to us, immersed as we are in this world. But it is real comfort. If only we could ask those who died in suffering, they would give us a glowing testimony from the heavenly point of view. After all, is not that world real and this one only a shadow?

GOD USES SUFFERING TO MOLD US

At this point we have a serious problem with the meaning of words. Take the word *discipline*. Our writer uses it ten times in 12:4–11. (The KJV uses *chastening*.) Ten times! It is almost impossible to read that word and feel positive about it. It is an emotional, painful word. Even though we must use the word *discipline* to translate the Greek word (because we have no other better), we still have visions of a good stout hickory switch across the back of the legs or the board of education applied to the seat of learning.

The fact that the word *punish* occurs alongside *discipline* (12:6) where our author quotes from Proverbs 3:12, doesn't help. But that word *punish* is translated *scourge* in the KJV and NASB, and is mistranslated in the NIV. It actually means "to afflict with disease or suffering." Nowhere else does it mean "to punish." In fact, if we turn back to Proverbs we discover that the word is not even in the verse—the writer of Hebrews quoted from the Septuagint (the oldest Greek version of the Old Testament).

Even though our English word *discipline* has connotations of punishment, the Greek word has no such connotation whatsoever. Rather, it is a positive word, if not a warm fuzzy word, that sums up the whole idea of loving parents teaching and training their children. It is a word from the world of education; it has to do with instilling the skills, abilities, and self-esteem that children need in order to mature. Yes, there is pain involved, but the pain comes from the outside; and the parent and the child are united in facing and dealing with it.

The writer of Hebrews chose to illustrate God's place in our suffering by drawing on our own experience as parents. First of all, good parents comfort their children when suffering strikes. God is a loving Father, and he always treats his children as beloved sons and daughters. I know very well that I am not going to try to make life difficult for my children. And you don't know any good parent who enjoys making life difficult for his children, do you? We have a term for cruel or sadistic parents: child abusers. That is against the law (God's law too!) and contrary to our understanding of true love.

Unlike our heavenly Father, we cannot foresee and intercept the suffering that comes into the lives of our children. But like him, we can—and do—stand with our sons and daughters in the hard times. When they come home bruised and emotionally battered because of ridicule or failure, we listen, we encourage, we touch and love them, we give counsel and advice, hoping that something we say or do will help them learn to cope with injury.

If we can be loving parents, how much more God can do! He listens and he is never preoccupied with other concerns. His counsel is sure, and his insight is truth. He not only listens to our words without condemnation, he reads our thoughts. His hand of healing reaches all the way to the hidden pain deep within us. But his discipline, as does ours, goes far beyond comfort.

God's loving discipline is also a matter of teaching. Teaching is the giving of necessary information. How are we to learn about the resources God has available? The best students are those who have been convinced that they really need what the teacher is offering. Until we know that we need God, we are not going to put ourselves out to learn from him. Not until we have exhausted every other option and mined every possible source of human wisdom, will we turn to learn of God. Why, oh why, is he always the refuge of last resort? To bring us to that place of teachableness, he filters the suffering that enters our lives. His only purpose is to direct our attention from ourselves and our paltry resources to his inexhaustible supply.

Finally, God's discipline includes training, changing harmful behavior to healthful behavior. Isn't is marvelous how well God knows us? He knows, for instance, that we are selfish and lazy. We are not going to do anything to make life difficult for ourselves. We will take the easy way out and slide along as far as we can. If he gave us a problem-free life, we would shrivel and die in our selfishness. We would curl in on ourselves. Why would any sane, sensible person wrestle with an invisible, transcendent God as long as human resources are sufficient?

We avoid change passionately because change is painful. The very first step in change is the painful recognition that we need to change, and that is a blow to our inflated egos. After that first shock, we work through the uncomfortable process of unlearning one habit and replacing it with another. Finally, we are ready to settle down in our new priorities—only to discover that more change is needed!

Will anything induce us to change except necessity? The pain of difficult circumstances must become so great that the pain of change seems the best way out. So our heavenly Father patiently arranges the circumstances to point us in his direction. If any other way were available, consistent with his character, to break us loose from the shackles of this earthly existence, God would use it.

The only other way to make us become what he designed us to be is not consistent with his character. One word—God could speak one word, and every last rebellious son and daughter of Adam would instantly become gentle and loving. Another word, and everyone would become generous and selfless. Yes, God could force us to become whatever he pleases; he has both the right and the power. But if he used that power, he would destroy the image of himself stamped upon us in creation. He gave us a will to choose, and he continues to give us, fallen though we are, grace that enables us to make a real choice. But he will not determine that choice. So he uses suffering to soften our thickened heads and break through our self-centered affections.

Our writer concluded with these words: "God disciplines us for our good, that we may share in his holiness." His whole purpose in the plan of redemption is to restore the companionship that rebellion destroyed in the Garden of Eden. Yet for us he is distant and unrelated, vague and incomprehensible. To bridge that distance, to bring us into his presence, he must provide a way to fit us and make us fit for his company. He will not force us, so he corrals us through our circumstances. His work is to prepare us to enjoy his presence, to enjoy the holiness and beauty and love of God. What he is doing in us is getting us fit for heaven. That is a very big job!

God knows exactly what it is going to take to prepare us for heaven. He will excise the selfishness of our hearts. He will allow us to be torn to pieces, if necessary, so that he can sift from our characters the sinful and earthy. He will mold us into those tender, mature, and loving persons that he designed us to be. He will crush the hardness and the callousness from our personalities. Through his discipline, he is trying to take from us those faults that limit our usefulness and joy here. And he does it by filtering the suffering in our lives.

This is a strange way to look at suffering because we instinctively run from pain. But when we view suffering through the eyes of God, it seems different. It doesn't make pain any less painful or any easier. Nor does it cause us to shed fewer tears or allow us to avoid grieving with broken hearts through sleepless nights.

Suffering is hard. It is perhaps impossible for us to understand the terrible damage that sin—Adam's sin—has wreaked on us. Sin has so warped and twisted our human nature that a loving God, seeking only our best, must allow hurt to break us before we will even consider his offer of companionship. Yet that is exactly our pitiful condition.

We can choose to rebel against the suffering and miss the comfort, teaching, and training of our Father's discipline. When suffering comes, we can raise our clenched fists and shout, "God, what do you think you are doing anyway? You can't do this to me!" We can complain and fret, grow bitter and hard. How many professing Christians hide a hard knot of bitterness down in their hearts because they feel that God has been unfair to them? Their worship is barren; their joy has evaporated; there is an irritable edginess in their voices. They have shut themselves off from the source of wisdom and comfort!

On the other hand, in the midst of pain and tears and

agony, we can bow our hearts and pray, "I cannot bear this alone. Will you bear it for me? Will you guard my attitudes and teach me to be like you through this trial?" When we bow in submission before our Father, with our hearts broken and our spirits crushed, our lives take on the holy sweetness of the presence of Christ.

Suffering will continue to come, whatever our choice. It will harden us or it will open to us a door into the presence of our Father. We decide. What is your choice?

As helpless as a child who clings
   Fast to his father's arm,
And casts his weakness on the strength
   That keeps him safe from harm:
So I, my Father, cling to thee,
   And thus I every hour
Would link my earthly feebleness
   To thine almighty power.

As trustful as a child who looks
   Up in his mother's face,
And all his little griefs and fears
   Forgets in her embrace:
So I to thee, my Savior, look,
   And in thy face divine
Can read the love that will sustain
   As weak a faith as mine.

As loving as a child who sits
   Close by his parent's knee,
And knows no want while he can have
   That sweet society:
So sitting at thy feet, my heart
   Would all its love outpour,
And pray that thou wouldst teach me, Lord,
   To love thee more and more.

                    James Drummond Burns

14

RUNNING THE RACE LAID OUT FOR US

Hebrews 12:1–3

The high school I attended had a five-year program, and eighth grade was the beginning of high school. It was also "try-out" year. Eighth graders could go out for any sport they chose, and they would be given a chance to train and play. No one would be cut or disqualified from his or her chosen team.

I had entered my adolescent growth spurt a little earlier than many of my classmates, and I had grown more than six inches in the previous year. I was the original prototype of the beanpole. If I turned sideways, I didn't even cast a shadow in bright sunlight. I had all the grace of a deer—a deer on ice. I was too chicken to play football, and I stumbled over my feet walking down the hall. So basketball was definitely out.

I decided that I would try track and field—the threat to my health and ego seemed more remote than in the other sports. So I ran, tried the broad jump, and even the hurdles. My lack of coordination was remarkable. But I tried. Or, to be honest, I tried up to a point.

My lack of coordination was one hindrance. But the more basic problem was my lack of motivation. I ran at school and in practice. But the other fellows on the team ran every day—before school or after school or both. I didn't really want to run. Needless to say, I didn't stay in track and field.

The underlying burden of this book is the fact that vast

numbers of evangelical Christians run only at church. The public image is polished; the glowing profession is couched in the right terms and phrases. But the motivation to put themselves out for the glory of God is missing. They are comfortable in their faith. They believe that a legal transaction in the past assures their salvation in the future, that token obedience is all that God requires, that their lukewarm discipleship harms no one but themselves.

Our Hebrew author chose the analogy of a footrace to teach us the nature of the Christian life. Against the radiant backdrop of the great cloud of witnesses (chapter 11), he turns to our personal race. Hebrews 12:1–17 stands out in the entire Bible as the most detailed outline of the Christian's life that I have found. Yet in the commentaries and studies this chapter has often been chopped into pieces, losing the central thread of continuity. Let me briefly outline it, and then in this and the following three chapters, I will break down the account into its parts.

RUNNERS ARE BEING SANCTIFIED

The fundamental idea of a race is that deliberate exertion is required to get from one place to another, and that the course and destination are clearly determined beforehand. There is always preparation (vv. 1–3), progress (vv. 4–11), and purpose (vv. 12–17). I discussed the discipline of *progress* in the last chapter, and I'll turn to *purpose* in later chapters. Right now let's deal with *preparation*.

If I were to ask modern evangelical Christians to summarize their understanding of the Christian life in one word, probably few would choose *progress* as that word. Words like *peace, love, hope, forgiveness, faith* would be the common ones. Few evangelicals think of Christian life in terms of continuing progress and change. The Reformed tradition teaches a progressive sanctification that is a gradual lifelong process of transformation of the believer's inward and outward life through the work of the Holy Spirit.

Those in the Wesleyan tradition, on the other hand,

emphasize an instantaneous sanctification followed by growth in grace throughout the remainder of one's life. In this second act of grace, subsequent to conversion, the affections and will of the believer are purified from sinful pride and self-will by the baptism of the Holy Spirit. Other traditions have a doctrine of sanctification, but none of us spends much time wrestling with it. That lack explains much about the shallowness and immaturity of American Christianity.

One of the great blessings that God has given his church is the fact that the Scriptures were written before we became polarized by our theological debates. Our Hebrew friend had no problems with progressive sanctification: that is the whole point of his analogy of the race. But neither did he have problems with instantaneous decisions and transformations; such experiences are an essential part of the preparation for the race.

WESLEY'S SYNTHESIS

John Wesley broke the ideas of sanctification down into three manageable parts, but he recognized that these parts overlapped and interlocked in the Scriptures.

First, he believed in progressive sanctification, which he usually termed "growth in grace." (He always preferred biblical terms over theological.) Like the author of Hebrews—as well as the rest of the New Testament—Wesley insisted that the whole of Christian experience was one continuous process of transformation, both in a believer's personal walk with God and in one's relationships with other believers.

Second, Wesley believed in what he termed "initial sanctification." This was one aspect of conversion. He was convinced that the new birth makes a dramatic change in a believer's life. Sinful actions and attitudes are transformed in an instant of time. Much remains to be done, but the Christian life begins with a clear break from the old life.

Finally, Wesley believed in—and preached—"entire sanctification." This is a spiritual crisis in the life of the believer who is being sanctified gradually, in which the issues of self-will and the lordship of Christ are settled. In the sense of a divided will united, or divided loyalties ended, Wesley preached the possibility of a pure heart. The surrender of self-will has profound impact in the life of the believer, and the evidences of that impact vary from person to person. So at times Wesley seemed to claim more for entire sanctification than he did at other times. But always he came back to the central issue of self-will. His Wesleyan followers have not been so wise.[1]

The race to which we are called by our Hebrew brother is actually, then, the continuing process of sanctification, a process that is punctuated by sanctifying events. This sanctifying work is the work of God—it is no more human effort than is our salvation. But, as with all analogies, this one has a limitation. In the race, the runners use their own strength to reach their goals. They have trained and prepared. They are dependent on their own physical and emotional resources. But that cannot be carried over into the spiritual race, though it seems that some teach sanctification as if it is our part of the bargain. Sanctification is God's work.

If we place sanctification in the context of grace and response, we find insight. Our relationship with God is based on his grace freely given to us and on our decision to obey him. He speaks—I respond. He leads—I follow. He disciplines—I yield. As I respond point by point, I find that there is order and progress in his dealings with me. I am becoming like Jesus Christ in my character and in my ministry.

COMPANIONSHIP AND USEFULNESS

Both personal and interpersonal aspects are part of this process. We evangelicals are most familiar with the personal aspect, which we usually call "growth in grace." (But we tend to mean less by this phrase than either Wesley or the Bible intends.) As we sit under the preaching and teaching of the Word, our knowledge increases. We learn to be faithful to the church, to behave as Christians. We learn to have confidence in God and become more stable. Our relationship with him becomes deeper and more satisfying. We begin to tell of our joy with those around us.

The disciplines of the spiritual life—prayer, Bible study, fellowship—touch initially the personal, inward parts of our lives. It has to be this way. The old adage is true: God calls us to *be* before he calls us to *do*. The believer who tries to serve God without learning to walk with him as an intimate companion is doomed to disappointment and failure. But (and that *but* should be printed in big, bright letters) growth in our individual spiritual lives is not all there is to sanctification.

The responsive believer is also making progress in becoming more and more useful in the kingdom of God. One who has been a Christian for ten years should be vastly more useful to the kingdom than one who has been a Christian only a few months. One who has walked with God for twenty or thirty years should have come to the place that his or her life is consumed in ministering to people both in and out of the fellowship of the church. Out of growing personal relationships with God, believers channel more and more of God's grace into the webs of relationships that the Spirit creates around them.

Henry Goodfellow was a young man, probably twenty-two or twenty-three years of age when he began to keep his diary in 1784. He was the son of an Irish gentleman, and already, at the beginning of the diary, Henry was chief constable, a position of some honor and influence. He had recently married and had just become a Christian under the preaching of the Methodists. Though his social class despised the Methodists, Henry soon joined with them.

He was converted in April 1784. He joined the Methodists in September. One month later he was hosting a class meeting in his home, thus publicly identifying himself with the Methodists. By December he was a member of a Methodist band. These were small groups of young men who covenanted with each other to watch over one another and challenge each other toward holiness of life.

By February 1785, he had become a prayer meeting leader in the cottages of his community. In June, only a little over a year after he was converted, he became a class leader. That made him one of the leaders of the Methodist society. In September 1785, he spoke publicly for the first time. And within three years he had become a regular local preacher, preaching several times each week.

Goodfellow represents hundreds of other Methodist converts whose diaries I have found. He not only grew as far as his relationship with God was concerned, but with every step that he made he was given (and accepted humbly) additional responsibility in ministry as well.

It is interesting to read of his response to these expanding opportunities. The day he led his first class meeting he was scared to death. But he commented afterward, "God blessed me." The first time he spoke in public was at a love feast. The diary entry gives the impression that Henry was shaking in his shoes, knees knocking. Yet he was compelled to speak because God had given him something to say.

We are in danger if we separate the personal and interpersonal aspects of running the race: we thwart the plan of God for the redemption of this world. We are chosen to be his agents and instruments to reveal God's love toward us. We are adopted into his family, with clear family responsibilities toward our brothers and sisters. For sublime reasons that we cannot fathom, God has chosen to work through us creatures, and there is much that God will not do without human instruments. God's church is not a waiting room; it is a body through which Christ is revealed to the world.

Emphasis on personal spiritual growth is one-sided, and the effects show up in many ways. The reluctance of "mature" Christians to witness actively for their Lord demonstrates a profound immaturity. The ease with which many Christians say "No" to new opportunities marks them as spiritual children. Though they have been Christians for years, every invitation to get involved is brushed aside. "I have never done that before" is the usual excuse, which should be followed by, "and I won't be bothered to try."

When someone responds to an invitation to serve God with, "I could never do that. That scares me," I am tempted to respond, "That is very good evidence that this is exactly what God wants you to do." If there is one thing that most of us avoid like the plague, it is being stretched. We don't like to be uncomfortable or feel inadequate. We don't like to be scared, with butterflies in the stomach. We don't like the fear that whispers in our ear, "Friend, you are about to make a fool of yourself!" So we back off, not wanting to lose face through a mistake or blunder, and say, "Oh, no, Lord. I'd rather be comfortable and satisfied."

Of course, combining personal and interpersonal growth is not easy—witness how nearly we have abandoned the effort. As I commented before, I suspect that deep down many Christians believe that God's plan for them is to make them happy and comfortable. My church, and most evangelical churches I know, are staffed by less than a third of the nominal members. A few committed Christians try to carry out the ministry that belongs to whole congregations. We elect them to do the job. The willingness—yes, the determination—of most of our members to be served rather than to serve is a telltale mark of our distance from God. In abandoning the clear and comprehensive preaching and teaching of sanctification, we have gutted the ministry of God's church in our world.

The second barrier to teaching our people to run the race is the fact that many believe that if they grow personally, God doesn't really care about the interpersonal aspect. If they are honest and faithful, well behaved, and loyal to the church, God will not require anything more of them. The tragedy is that in seeking personal growth apart from service, we grow stale and stagnant. Even though we may seek his presence and companionship, he is not to be found. He does rejoice in our worship and our fellowship, but his heart is out there with those who hurt and wander in the dark. If we will not go with him out there, he cannot come to us in our spiritual disciplines.

THE PROBLEM OF THE WILL

The author of this epistle brings us face to face with the problem of the human will—again. The word *lay aside* is an active verb. It means to take off and lay down, literally as I would take off my coat and lay it aside. The long tunics and robes that were the usual dress for men in the ancient world were not designed for running. Neither were the sandals they wore. Preparation for a race involved laying aside the outer garments, kicking off the sandals, and gathering the inner garments to be secured by the sash around the waist.

Our Hebrew writer used this analogy of preparation in two ways. First, we are to lay aside "everything that hinders" and, second, "the sin that so easily entangles us." Both phrases refer to God's work of sanctifying the believer. This epistle was written to Christians, to born-again believers. So this passage does not refer to conversion. That experience establishes a relationship with God, and lays the foundation for God to begin his sanctifying work.

"Everything that hinders" is a very broad category that is uniquely personal to each of us. None of us will be asked to lay aside the same hindrances, for what hinders me may actually spur you on. The desire that pushes for first place in my life may have no appeal for you whatsoever. I understand only partially how that applies to me at this particular moment, and I certainly cannot apply it to you.

If God merely led us in paths compatible with our own desires, then sanctification would be no problem for any of us. Nor would we have problems if God in an act of sovereign power caused us to desire what he wills. But in his gift of freedom he does neither. Every believer experiences—from the very beginning of the relationship with God—the painful truth that God's will crosses human desire almost daily.

Often we face cross-purposes with God over good and proper things of life. Material possessions may be a point of conflict. God may well confront our desire for a larger home with the need for a new church in Africa. He might ask for that long-awaited vacation to be used for a work mission to build that church. Personal ambitions are good, but God may ask us to forego the coveted promotion to give more time to discipling young Christians. Even our families may be sources of tension when God calls the children into full-time ministry instead of the family business. At each of these points of confrontation with God, the responsive heart "lays aside" personal preference.

Our most difficult choices are between the good and the

best. We must be sensitive to God to avoid settling for the merely good. It is not possible to enjoy to the fullest everything good that our material civilization offers and still serve Jesus Christ. We don't have the time or the energy. There will be many times that we must lay aside the good in order to respond to the gentle grace of our Father.

Some who have maintained a strong emphasis on sanctification have fallen into the trap of asceticism at this point. Asceticism is self-denial for the sake of appearances. God will call all maturing Christians to forego legitimate pleasures to free time or resources for his service. Responsive, growing Christians do so gladly, though not without an occasional, often painful, struggle. But it is easy to run ahead of God. If God calls us to deny ourselves certain pleasures from time to time, we will deny ourselves other, or all, pleasures all the time to prove our dedication to God. But as far as obedience is concerned, it is just as willful to go beyond what God asks as to refuse him, if by our denial we call attention to ourselves. What disguises spiritual pride can assume!

Sanctification cannot, then, be reduced (or expanded!) to a code of "do's" or "do-withouts." This is true—and we go back to where we started—simply because sanctification is the work of God, not ours. The only responsibility we have in this companionship with God is to respond to his initiatives. The Pharisees of Jesus' day were not evil men, as the world defines evil. But they had long since stopped responding to God's initiatives and had set out on their own to do the work of God. And in the end it was they, not the criminals and prostitutes, who crucified Jesus.

At each point so far, we have faced the problem of our human will, or, to be more precise, the problem of our self-will, our willfulness. The second phrase instructs us to "lay aside the sin that so easily entangles us." The KJV translates that "the sin that besets," and we have turned that around into "the besetting sin." Then we have applied it to those problems or weaknesses that each of us is particularly liable to. Some might say that overeating is their besetting sin; other might name smoking or lust. But these miss the point altogether.

The writer refers again to the long, full robes and tunics. If a man tried to run without preparing himself, the folds of cloth would wrap themselves around his legs and probably trip him up. The phrase does not suggest a specific sin so much as it suggests sin in a much more general sense, something that confronts all of us. Can we lay our finger on a universal problem that prevents Christians from running the race that is laid out for them?

I believe we can, and we can do it without using theological terms like "original sin" or "native depravity." It is really very simple. The sin that so easily entangles us is the choice we make to place reservations on our service to Jesus Christ. It is the act of our will that announces to God, "I will run so far and no farther." "I'll go to church, but don't ask me to do anything because I'm too busy." "Don't ask me to be a witness or teacher or accept that call or live in that community or take that cut in salary or. . . ."

Reservations on doing the whole will of God come in infinite variety. But every reservation is still an entanglement. It reminds me of the high school basketball player who has fallen in love with that special girl. She is sitting in the bleachers three rows up. He has his eye on his girl. All the time he is not actually holding the ball, he is watching her out of the corner of his eye to see whether she is watching him. You know what kind of ballgame he will play! He will make bad mistakes and miss good opportunities to score. He will let his team, his coach, his girl, and himself down hard. He cannot play ball because he will not play without reservations.

Our Hebrew author goes further. Before we can run the race laid out for us, we have to deal with the reservations and the self-will that lie behind them. This, too, is part of God's sanctifying work. The laying aside of our reservations literally gets to the core of our human personalities. Whether we interpret sanctification as functional (to set apart solely for the service of God) or moral (to purify and make fit for the service of God), we must deal with a selfish, I-want-my-own-way will.

God asks every believer to yield his or her will to him. Fully. Completely. Forever. We cannot make the choice quickly or casually. In his faithfulness he will draw us step by step and closer and closer to the heart of the issue, gradually sanctifying us at each confrontation. He will prepare us, if we are responsive, to make a conscious and intelligent choice to surrender totally to his will and pleasure. Simple. Profound. Far-reaching. Essential. This is "laying aside the sin that so easily entangles us."

Lest you charge me with some horrible form of perfectionism, let me assure you that this is not the end of God's sanctifying work. Remember, this is preparation for the race and not part of the race itself. Yet to come, as God continues progressively to sanctify us, is the trial of suffering, the fatherly discipline, the expanded ministry, the burden of responsibilities. At each step of life, whatever God chooses to make of us, our companionship with a holy God demands a constantly responsive heart.

> Spirit of God, descend upon my heart;
> Wean it from earth; through all its pulses move;
> Stoop to my weakness, mighty as thou art,
> And make me love thee as I ought to love.
>
> Hast thou not bid me love thee, God and King?
> All, all thine own, soul, heart and strength and mind.
> I see thy cross; there teach my heart to cling:
> O let me seek thee, and O let me find!
>
> Teach me to love thee as thine angels love,
> One holy passion filling all my frame;
> The baptism of the heaven-descended Dove,
> My heart an altar, and thy love the flame.
>
> George Croly

NOTE

[1] Wesley's *A Plain Account of Christian Perfection* is a good and precise, if disjointed, summary of his position. *The Works of John Wesley,* 14 vols. (Grand Rapids: Zondervan [from 1872 London edition]), 11:366–448.

15

RUNNING THE RACE WITH THE WEAK

Hebrews 12:12–13

Sooner or later every weakness in our theology shows up in our songbook. Read carefully this verse written by J. E. Rankin, and see whether you can spot a problem.

> Are you weary, are you heavy-hearted?
> Tell it to Jesus, tell it to Jesus.
> Are you grieving over joys departed?
> Tell it to Jesus alone.

This song—and at least four others in the same collection—projects a serious, even devastating, message about the church of Jesus Christ. Rankin lists, in the entire song, the six most serious crises of our lives: discouragement, grief, sorrow, death, guilt, anxiety. Then he gives us the final solution: "Tell it to Jesus alone." That says to me, "In the crisis, don't involve anyone else. Be strong. If your faith is strong enough, you and God can work it out by yourselves."

Alone? Where did we ever get the idea that God expects his children to face the trials of life isolated from their brothers and sisters? What about this line from Haldor Lillenas' song: "How can I be lonely, when I've Jesus *only*?" Or James Rowe's statement, "Jesus is *all I need*." E. A. Hoffman closed the song "I Must Tell Jesus" with the line, "Jesus can help me, Jesus *alone*." (The emphases here are mine.) The point these poets were trying to make is that Jesus Christ is the one unfailing, totally faithful friend that we have. But I also see a vexing assumption: the only help troubled Christians can (or should) expect from God is direct, individual support.

That assumption is not biblical. In fact, I find the Bible teaching us that the fellowship of Christians is the first and primary channel God uses to give us strength when we are weak or in need. It is exactly at these times of crisis that we most need the loving touch, the encouraging word, the emotional support of Christians. Why at these points of crisis should we not tell the church about our need?

There is another song that was a favorite with gospel quartets when I was growing up.

> On the Jericho Road, there is room for just two.
> No more and no less, just Jesus and you.
> Each burden he'll bear, each sorrow he'll share.
> There's never a care, for Jesus is there.

It is simply not true. I find nowhere that Jesus walked the Jericho Road with only one disciple. On the Jericho Road, and on every pathway of life, there is room for Jesus and you and me and the whole redeemed family of God, every man and woman who loves Jesus Christ. We are not in a solitary race. We are not alone. Not only is God with us every step, we are in the company of fellow Christians. God never intended that we should fight our battles by ourselves, that we should have to handle the conflicts of life and pretend to be strong.

After placing so much emphasis on companionship with God, it may seem that I am now contradicting myself. But the fact is—and I shall return to this fact in the next chapter—that companionship with God automatically involves, even requires, companionship with the children of God. Sin is divisive and alienating; godliness is uniting and cohesive. Inevitably, the person who is drawn to God is also drawn to the fellowship of Christian companions.

THE CHURCH IS RESPONSIBLE
FOR WEAK MEMBERS

The writer of Hebrews brings us face to face with this reality. On the heels of his paragraph about the loving discipline of our Father, he turns to three significant statements about the responsibilities of God's church. These three statements will be the topics of this and the two succeeding chapters. Hebrews 12:12–13 is a statement about the church and human weakness. Verse 14 is a statement about the church and godly relationships. Verses 15-17 are a statement about the church and Christian accountability.

Our writer exhorted his readers to "strengthen [their] feeble arms and weak knees," to "make level paths for [their] feet, so that the lame man not be disabled, but rather be healed" (12:12–13).

The passage is a difficult one to translate, and it is far more difficult if we fail to realize that there is a distinct transition between verses 11 and 12. Our Hebrew author moves very quickly from the problem of God's discipline of the individual Christian to believers' responsibility for one another. The two ideas are certainly related but distinct. God uses suffering to sanctify us, and he uses the church as his channel of help. Through the fellowship of believers God comforts, strengthens, teaches, and trains the individual Christian.

A few observations about the verses themselves are in order before we go on. The NIV places emphasis on the personal pronoun *your:* "your feeble arms and weak knees." Actually, *your* does not occur in that phrase, but does occur in the next phrase: "level paths for your feet." It is a plural pronoun, that could be best translated by a southern "you all!" In the last phrase the NIV indicates that *lame* refers to a lame person, where the NASB suggests, by supplying the word *limb,* that the writer is referring to a believer's own weakened body. To whose arms and knees is the writer referring?

In fact, it seems clear that the writer has in mind the feeble members of the Hebrew church, whom the rest had the responsibility to protect and encourage. The Living Bible almost captures the point: "Mark out a straight, smooth path for your feet so that those who follow you, though weak and lame, will not fall and hurt themselves, but become strong." If we substitute *accompany* for *follow*, we come closer: "Those who accompany you."

ALL CHRISTIANS ARE SOMETIMES WEAK

If we make these verses an exhortation for believers to strengthen themselves, we do a grave injustice to those who happen to be weak among us. The plain truth is that it isn't easy to take charge of difficult circumstances and to strengthen oneself. How often do we find that when we are weak we actually lack not only the strength but also the will to take charge? I know what happens when I don't feel good. I know very well that a long list of chores await my attention, but I don't want to do them. I don't feel like doing them, and I bury my head in a pillow (or a book).

Weakness means that we lack both the strength and the will to do what we ought to do. It doesn't help for some well-meaning saint to come along and say, "Pull yourself together. If you pray about it, everything is going to work out. Smile, now, and get a move on." It is at those points of difficulty and fear that we need a helping hand, a listening ear, an understanding heart to strengthen us. We don't need advice; we need a brother or sister to share the burden, who will take some of the load off our shoulders.

I have heard messages about how God took care of poor discouraged Elijah in the desert. (In fact, I have preached some.) An angel came straight from the throne of God and ministered to him. He cooked a meal for Elijah, not once but twice. Wouldn't it be grand if an angel came to help us when we were weak? Or maybe it wouldn't be so grand because it would rob us of the opportunity to experience the loving touch of our brothers and sisters. After all, angels don't stay around long enough for us to get very well acquainted.

Why did God send an angel to help Elijah? After reading the story many times, I realized that Elijah wasn't supposed to be in the desert in the first place. God didn't lead him there. He had run from trouble and discouragement because he was overcome by fear. By heading out into the desert, he had deliberately isolated himself from all those people in the land who were faithful to God. I'm sure that most of those 7,000 faithful believers would gladly have taken care of Elijah if they had been given opportunity, the fury of the queen notwithstanding. But he didn't bother to give them the opportunity. He took off for the desert.

We do the same thing. When we get discouraged and burdened and feel like quitting the human race, we take off for the desert. And out there we wonder, "Where are God and his angels?" We don't realize that we left all the angels back at the church, in our church family. God does not usually send angels, though in Elijah's case he made an exception, perhaps because Elijah had run so far that his life was in danger. But God's ordinary method of helping us is his children, his family. It is among believers that we find strength when we are weak, encouragement when we fail, help when we are in trouble— where we find people who will love us when we don't even like ourselves.

This is the pastoral work of the church—it is the work of God. He didn't bring us together in order for us to put on our best faces on Sunday morning and come to church looking successful. The church is a ministry of Christian to Christian, meeting each other at their common points of need. It is not our holiness that binds us together nor our right theology nor our gifts and abilities. God brings us together because of our own need—the points where we are weak and where we fail.

GOD CALLS US IN OUR WEAKNESS

These verses translate into two lessons that every American Christian needs to learn, and learn well. The first is this: *When you are down, expect God to strengthen you through fellow Christians.*

I suppose it is the most natural thing in the world—in this world—to hide when we are weak and strut when we are strong. But to hide from other believers is to cut ourselves off from healing. We cannot fully understand the way (or the why) God uses suffering to cause us to mature. Nor can we fully understand why he has chosen to heal our injuries and weaknesses through the fellowship of Christians rather than in direct, individual encounters. But the Scriptures make it clear: that is his choice. If we are to experience his healing, we must be open to one another.

The second lesson is the other side of the coin. *If we are to be children of God, we are going to have to look for opportunities to help one another.* We will have to go out of our way to help the weak, the faltering, the discouraged. There are profound social implications in this, and I am aware of the needs of the disadvantaged and powerless in our society. But if we will not reach out to fellow members of the household of faith, we will never be able to address the needs in our world effectively.

Jesus understood this. After all, he not only created the church but our human personalities as well. He placed special emphasis, in the hours just before his death, on the love that would distinguish the fellowship of Christians from all other associations. "By this all men will know that you are my disciples, if you love one another" (John 13:35). It is not love generated by human compassion, but the love of God—God himself—taking up residence in our lives. Perhaps there is no way that modern Christians demonstrate their distance from God more than in their attitude toward fellow believers. May God have mercy on us.

I have a growing appreciation for Jesus' account of the final judgment in Matthew 25. Upon the goats on his left hand, he pronounced doom. They had failed to provide him with food, water, clothing, and companionship in his hour of need. They had failed to shelter him and visit him in prison. Shocked, they asked, "Lord, when did we see you hungry or thirsty or a stranger or needing clothes or sick or in prison, and did not help you?" He replied, "Whatever you did not do for one of the least of these, you did not do for me" (vv. 31–46).

To the sheep on his right hand, he issues the glorious invitation to join him in heaven. They had ministered to him in

many ways. But the righteous were also shocked. "When did
we minister to you in these ways?" Jesus responded, again,
"Whatever you did for one of the least of these brothers of
mine, you did for me." These believers had been ministering to
the weak and broken without fully knowing what they were
doing. They had ministered, not because it earned them credit,
but because the love of God constrained them. They were
channels through which the grace of God continually poured
into the cursed world in which they lived.

I have looked for a modern-day analogy or parallel that
could serve as a model of the church in action. The biblical
analogy of the body is effective; but until we see it in action, it is
not compelling. I think I have found it. I attended my first
Alcoholics Anonymous meeting recently. I found a room full of
men, women, and youth drawn together by their need, not
their success.

The speaker of the evening closed with the question that
had been asked of him ten years earlier. "Do you believe that
these people could help you stay sober?" At the time he did not
believe in God or any other higher power, but he did see in the
group individuals who were taking charge of their lives and
defeating the power of drink. "Yes," he responded. And in
making that commitment, he not only found freedom, he found
God. He told us so in plain English. Now he—once a violent,
unrepentant, arrogant drunk—was offering himself to others
who wanted freedom. That, my friend, is the way every church
ought to function.

Reuben Welch relates the following story in his fascinating
study of First John, entitled *We Really Do Need Each Other*.[1] I
am going to repeat it in his own special style.

At school a few years ago

there was a summer school course in "Group and
                                   Interpersonal
                                   Relations."
About a dozen people took the class
and at the end of it
    they decided they wanted to do something

together
as a kind of closing to the class.
You know,
they had come to know each other,
and to share with each other,
and really be personal to each other
and break down walls
and so forth—
so they decided to get together and take a hike
up to Hennigar Flats.
Now, Hennigar Flats is about three miles
up the side of the mountain behind the campus
and it takes about an hour and a half
for anyone to walk up there.

So they set the day
and made the sandwiches
and made the chocolate
and brought the cold drinks
and the back packs
and they got all gathered up for the safari
and they started up the mountain—
together.
But it wasn't long until
the strong, stalwart ones were up in front and
the other ones were back in the middle and
way back at the end of the line
was a girl named Jane—
who was, you might say,
out of shape.
At the front was Don—
a big, strong, former paratrooper.
He and some others—the strong ones—
were up in front and
the weak ones were back in the back and
way in the back
was Jane.
And Don said—
it was he who told me the story—
He looked back a couple of switchbacks
and saw Jane
and the Lord told him
That he had just better go back
and walk with her.
That's kind of hard on him because he has a need to be
first.

But he went down
  and started walking with Jane
  and the people in the level above called down,
              "Come on up.
                It's great up here."
          And Jane yelled, "I don't think I can
                make it."
          And they hollered, "Yeah, you can.
                Try harder, come on up."
          And every time they called to her
          down went her own sense of worth
          down went her own sense of value—
              "I can't make it."
              "Oh, yeah, you can. Come on."

So the strong went on ahead
  and the weak hung behind
    and here was Jane
      and she never made it to the top.

Now look what you have.
You have a group—
            we know each other
            we like each other
            we want to do this together
            let's go to Hennigar Flats together.
    But before long, you have divided
        the strong and the weak
        the haves and the have-nots
    and the ables and the unables.
          So what started out as a group
          has now become a fragmented collection.
And so the strong say,
            "You can do it."
And the weak say,
            "No, I can't."
And so the strong say
            "Try harder"—
            which is a big help.
That's a big help.
          And she didn't make it.
Thankfully, that's not the last chapter.

    They must have learned their lessons
      because they decided that was no way
        to end the fellowship of that class
          and they got together and decided

to do it again.
But they made some new rules—
it was everybody go
or nobody go
and they were all going
together.
So they set the day
and made the sandwiches
and made the chocolate
and brought the cold drinks
and the back packs
and they got all gathered up
for the safari.
It took them four hours to make it to the top,
and the water was all gone
and the cold drinks were all gone
and the sandwiches were all gone
and the chocolate was all gone
and the back packs were empty
but they all made it,
together.

. . . .

You know something—
we're all just people who need each other.
We're all learning
and we've all got a long journey ahead of us
We've got to go together
and if it takes us until Jesus comes
we better stay together
we better help each other.
And I dare say
That by the time we get there
all the sandwiches will be gone
and all the chocolate will be gone
and all the water will be gone
and all the backpacks will be empty.
But no matter how long it takes us
We've got to go together.
Because that's how it is in the body of Christ.

*   *   *

Let us pray together.

Make us, O God, a church that shares
Thy love for all mankind;
That lives the truth thy Word declares,
And heeds the Master's mind.
Helps us reach out with loving hands,
In times that try the soul,
With sympathy that understands
And makes the needy whole.

Make us, O God, a church that cares
For every human need;
That suffers when one life despairs,
And moves to intercede.
Give to our voice prophetic power
That stirs each wavering heart
To meet the challenge of this hour
And take a noble part.

Make us, O God, a church that dares
Courageously to act;
That clothes with flesh its fervent prayers
And makes the gospel fact.
Now thrust us from the cloistered halls
Where fearful souls might hide,
And send us forth where duty calls
To serve the Crucified!

H. Victor Kane[2]

NOTES

[1] This story is taken from *We Really Do Need Each Other* by Reuben
Welch, pp. 106–10. Copyright © 1973 by Impact Books, assigned to the
Zondervan Corporation in 1982. Used by permission.

[2] Copyright © 1971 by the Hymn Society of America, Texas Christian
University, Fort Worth, TX 76129; reprinted under license no. 7240.

16

RUNNING THE RACE
COMMITTED TO PEACE

Hebrews 12:14

Imagine that we are standing in heaven before the throne of God, surrounded by a sea of happy people. (I can't really imagine it—but I can pretend.) For a moment we take our eyes off Jesus and look around us. We are struck immediately by the sheer diversity of the folks there. Every race, color, and culture is represented. Each person is unique in form and appearance. We are no more alike here in heaven than we were on earth.

Around us are Africans, Chinese, Polynesians, Eskimos, Indians; all are joining in enthusiastic worship. Western Christians, accustomed to orderly worship, merge joyfully into the throngs of singing saints who never saw an order of service on earth. We are amazed to realize that Christianity made none of these Christians like us!

The diversity astounds us, but after a moment's reflection, we are more astonished by a sense that something familiar is missing. As we look from face to glowing face, studying the radiant joy in each, we slowly understand that amid the diversities here, there are no barriers. No distance separates one person from another. These brothers and sisters are as close to each other—and to us—as the closest ties of blood that bound them together on earth. They are one huge family, totally and completely united, awash in the perfect love that marks the presence of God.

Yes, the familiar barriers are missing. Language, education, culture, intellectual ability, wealth, political status—not a trace is to be found here. And neither are there the personal barriers so familiar to us on earth. The radiant countenances reveal no hint of resentment, petty jealousy, unforgotten injuries, or selfish ambitions. Nothing clouds the companionship of these saints. Husbands and wives are not married here, but their relationship is far closer than they ever experienced on earth. The generation gap is, of course, nonexistent, for the terms of age have no meaning here.

You and I are so accustomed to the ever-present pain of strained relationships that a world without them is almost incomprehensible. But there will be perfect peace among all those who enter the pearly gates. Over there we will enjoy eternal life with unlimited relationships with God and all redeemed humanity. We shall walk the streets of glory and see people we have known here and millions more that we could never have known. We all will be the closest of friends, for there are no barriers.

Heaven is a place of peaceful diversity. That should not startle us: it is only a reflection of the personality of God himself. He has revealed himself to us as a trinity. On one hand, he is one God who exists in perfect unity. The Old Testament rings with the prophetic proclamation: "Hear O Israel: The Lord our God, the Lord is one" (Deut. 6:4). Standing in contrast to the thousands of pagan deities, God in perfect unity is one God. There are no divisions or parts in him. He is the same everywhere at all times. There is nothing about him that seems out of context with the rest of him. He is perfect oneness.

On the other hand, he reveals himself in three distinct personalities. In creation God said, "Let us make man in our image," a plural name for God with plural pronouns. Yet among those three personalities, no division exists. God the Father, Son, and Holy Spirit act in perfect agreement, total cooperation, and shared purpose. There is no hint of misunderstanding. He is perfect unity, yet a diversity of personality.

It is not surprising, then, that when God created us in his own image, he stamped us with both diversity and a profound need for relatedness. Individuals that we are, it is still essential for our physical and emotional health to belong, to be a part of a family, a group. It is the image of God stamped on the core of our being. By creation, then, we are wrapped in a web of relationships that reflect the nature of God. One God in three persons is reflected in God's plan of redemption: one church composed of a vast variety of personalities.

BROKEN RELATIONSHIPS
ALWAYS INVOLVE SIN

If relatedness is so basic to our personality, we can understand why the breaking of relationships is so devastating. The jilted teenager pines; the betrayed spouse falls to pieces; the estranged employee is frustrated and inefficient. Those who deliberately shut themselves away from meaningful contact we diagnose as mentally ill. The uncontrollable felon in solitary confinement promises anything in order to be returned to human company. The breaking of relationships causes the most intense emotional pain that can come to a human personality.

Broken relationships are abnormal to the human spirit. We cannot ever become desensitized to that pain. And every broken relationship is a direct or indirect result of sin. Sin, by its very nature, is divisive. Rebelliousness always separates. Adam's rebellion separated him and all his descendants from God. Our inherited willful nature also becomes a wedge that drives itself between God and us and those around us.

If heaven is a place of perfect relationship, then by contrast, hell must be the opposite—the absence of relationships. Perhaps in describing hell as a place of total darkness, Jesus was pointing out that awful aloneness is characteristic of the place of torment. The ultimate impact of sin is to separate us from God, to undermine human relationships, and finally to drive us to an eternal aloneness— an utter and total aloneness.

Wherever there is a broken relationship there is sin: in attitude, in action, in thought, in word, in omission. Marriages don't accidentally fall apart—they are destroyed by sin. Parents and children don't just happen to fall out. The wedges that drive

them apart are born in sin. Friendships don't just fracture by
themselves. They are fractured by sin. Congregations don't
split in God's plan. They are split by either self-seeking or self-
righteous people. At times innocent people suffer the impact of
the sins of others close to them; more often sin is found on all
sides of broken relationships.

God designed us for close relationships with himself and
our human family. Sin is a moral solvent that eats away at every
relationship. Against these realities, our Hebrew brother's
second statement about the heart of God's church reads, "Make
every effort to live in peace [pursue peace, NASB] with all men
and to be holy; without holiness no one will see the Lord"
(12:14).

THE PURSUIT OF PEACE AND HOLINESS

The word *pursue* (*follow,* KJV) means exactly what it says:
"to seek with great earnestness, to extend one's self in order to
grasp or obtain." Here is a wholehearted commitment to
achieve or grasp a goal. We have read all kinds of rags-to-riches
stories in which a disadvantaged young man or woman
purposed to be successful. And at the end of the story we have a
Henry Ford or an Andrew Carnegie. We understand what it
means to set our hearts on a goal and to devote all our energies
to reach that goal. We do not wait for it to come to us.

Two Greek words can be translated *with*. If this verse
contained the more common word, it would mean that we are
to seek a peaceful relationship with each and every individual
around us. That would make a true statement. But a different
word is used here. The verse actually commands us to "pursue
peace along with or alongside all people." God saves us
individually, then welds us together into the body of Christ, his
church. The command to pursue peace is a command given to
the church as a body, believers working side by side.

The writer of Hebrews has drawn together in one sentence
two dimensions of our lives that we evangelical Christians tend
to keep apart. He has joined together a personal relationship
with God and the interpersonal web of relationships with other

people. At the same time that we pursue a relationship with God, we are commanded to pursue peaceful relationships with our brothers and sisters as well as with non-Christians.

Some Christians in modern America seem to believe that so long as they have a religious experience, then nothing else ultimately matters. They can in fact be saved and at the same time hang on to resentment and bitterness, and sow dissension and ill will among the people around them. They can be selfish, petty, and demanding, creating havoc at home, at church, and at the office; and God will finally overlook it all because they have had a religious experience.

We cannot, however, enter heaven with the hostilities, anger, and fractured relationships that too many of us carry around in our hearts here. If we expect to step inside that gate, unload our bundles of hard feelings, and begin to enjoy the peace and wholeness of heaven, we face great disappointment. Broken relationships have no place in heaven. If they have no place there, then they have no place here, especially in God's church. God calls us to seek peace, to face the sin that causes division, and together find the healing of God.

The sanctification we are to pursue is the work of the grace of God, delivering us from that baggage here and now. The word denotes a process. It refers to the continuing encounter between God's grace and our wills that I have been describing throughout this book. It is the work of God in us that leads us toward maturity. It is his work that draws us into closer and deeper companionship with him. It is his transforming presence that makes us more and more useful in the kingdom. It is the discipline through which he comforts, teaches, and trains us.

JESUS CALLS US TO RADICAL FORGIVENESS

This command adds one new element to our understanding of God's sanctifying work. We are commanded to pursue this sanctifying grace, for without this transforming process, we will never see God. We do not merely wait for God to do something to us; in response to his grace we actively engage ourselves to search out peaceful relationships. This pursuit demands, first, that we deal with our own attitudes and, second, that we take the initiative to restore our broken relationships with other people.

The gospel confronts us with radical demands concerning forgiveness. Jesus taught us to pray, "Forgive us our trespasses, as we forgive those who trespass against us." To drive the point home, Jesus repeated it two sentences later. "For if you forgive men when they sin against you, your heavenly Father will also forgive you. But if you do not forgive men their sins, your Father will not forgive your sins" (Matt. 6:12, 14–15).

Many react vehemently against Jesus' demand for radical forgiveness. The opposition almost always boils down to the fact that the offender does not deserve forgiveness—he (or she) ought to have to suffer as he (she) has caused others to suffer. But once the truth is out, we hang our heads in shame, for down deep we know that *we* do not deserve forgiveness either. As God pours his mercy on us, so we must be merciful to the most wretched of enemies.

Corrie ten Boom relates the first post-war encounter she had with one of her former Nazi concentration camp guards. She was speaking in a church service in Munich, West Germany, when she recognized him, and the awful memories of that dehumanizing "processing center" at Ravensbrück flooded back. She and her sister Betsy, with hundreds of others, were forced to strip naked before jeering guards, and this man stood over them at the showers.

After the service, the former SS guard approached her and said, "How grateful I am for your message, Fräulein. To think that, as you say, God has washed my sins away!" Corrie could not respond to his outstretched hand. Angry, vengeful thoughts boiled through her mind. She prayed for strength to forgive him, but still her hand remained at her side. Finally, in desperation she prayed again, "Jesus, I cannot forgive him. Give me Your forgiveness."

Corrie continues:

As I took his hand the most incredible thing happened. From my shoulder along my arm and my hand a current seemed to pass from me to him, while into my heart sprang a love for this stranger that almost overwhelmed me. And so I discovered that it is not on our forgiveness any more than on our goodness that the world's healing hinges, but on His. When He tells us to love our enemies, He gives, along with the command, the love itself.[1]

Forgiveness is not complete, however, as long as silence reigns. The injury must usually be acknowledged and forgiveness either spoken or embodied in deliberate action. Somewhere along the line many of us have bought the idea that the way to pursue peace in the church is to keep our mouths shut. As far as gossip is concerned, that is true. But as far as building peaceful relationships, it is false, False, FALSE!

I spent the early years of my ministry keeping my mouth shut (as I had been taught) about anything that I thought might arouse a negative response from someone else. In plain English, I avoided anything remotely resembling a confrontation. I never spoke my mind; I couched every conversation in language I thought would be acceptable to my companions. I went to great pains to say what I thought others wanted to hear, even to the point of compromising the truth.

I even tackled conflict in my church by telling both parties what they wanted to hear. (Everyone wants to be told that he is right and the other party is wrong.) I tried to forgive those who hurt or criticized or ignored me; I really, honestly tried. But I would not address the cause of the pain because I would never tell the whole truth if there was a hint of anything negative. All the time, I considered my restraint to be "spiritual."

I am aghast at the damage I inflicted on myself, my wife, and my congregations by my commitment to "diplomacy." I grow every day more aware of the devastation being wrought in our churches by Christians—pastors and laity alike—who have never learned to speak the truth in love. As contradictory as it may sound, the only path I have found to truly peaceful, wholesome relationships among Christians is the path of honest, open confrontation.

I am working to make it my practice to confront face to

face in private those who criticize or oppose me. I approach every such encounter with fear and trembling; they never become any less painful. But confrontation is essential in Christian relationships for several reasons. First, Jesus himself demanded it: "If you are offering your gift at the altar and there remember that your brother has something against you, leave your gift there in front of the altar. First go and be reconciled to your brother; then come and offer your gift" (Matt. 5:23–24). God cares a great deal about broken relationships. In fact, he cares as much about our relationships with one another as about our relationship with him.

Second, I can learn about myself best from those who criticize me. My admirers (and I have a few, thank God!) praise me and tell me of my strengths. But only from my critics can I understand my faults and failures. I wish all my critics loved me the way Christians should, for "wounds from a friend can be trusted" (Prov. 27:6). But they don't. That is their problem, though, not mine. Even when the criticism is biting, bitter, and unfair, I can turn it over to my Father, who sorts the wheat from the chaff. If I am to continue to stretch toward maturity, I must understand my weakness.

Third, my friends have a right to understand me. As a Christian brother, I am called to contribute to their spiritual growth, regardless of our disagreements. It is in my honest expression of my feelings and my understandings that God may be able to teach them a lesson that they need. Perhaps, because of my courage in confronting the point of conflict, the Holy Spirit will release them from some restrictive misunderstanding or mistake.

Fourth, as a servant of Jesus Christ, I have no personal agenda to achieve. I have no business being concerned about the success of my program or completion of my plan. I do not need to twist arms or force compliance. God has called me only to be myself with my own personal set of gifts, points of view, and insights. Every other Christian brother and sister has a complementary set of gifts, points of view, and insights. I have no right to impose my view on my brother; neither do I have any right to silence him by my authority or self-defense. Until we as Christians get off our little ego trips (about being right all the time) and our personal kingdom-building (where we think we are in charge), we will never learn to find the will of God for his church. God is slowly bringing me to the place where I honestly do not want to have my way: I want God to have his way. Since he chooses to reveal part of his plan to me and part to a fellow believer (even if both of us seem cantankerous to the other), I am obligated by my commitment to God to sort through the conflicts until the pieces fit together.

It is in the confrontation between contrary opinions that God reveals to us both his will and our ignorance. There is not a Christian alive who cannot contribute to my life and ministry some important insight or gem of holiness. If I go through life reacting in anger to those who disagree with me, I shall miss many, maybe most, of God's greatest blessings. Where I choose to be defensive (and I still do at times, I admit) I close a door to the work of God in my life, and I destroy an opportunity that God has arranged to use me to build up a member of his family.

Forgiveness, then, becomes a dynamic process of facing and working through the conflicts in our relationships. Forgiveness is not sweeping the conflicts under the carpet and pretending that they do not exist "for the sake of the kingdom." It is learning to speak the truth in love. Forgiveness then becomes mutual. Each forgives the other for his part in the conflict, and together we step closer to the heart of God.

RESTORATION CAN BE BLOCKED

But learning to speak the truth in love will not solve all conflicts and restore all relationships, even among professing Christians. Sin, self-will, and pride will at times block our most humble and loving initiatives. Suppose my overtures are spurned; the other party does not respond. What then?

In Matthew 18:15–17, Jesus gives us three simple steps for dealing with broken relationships. This passage has been used for centuries to support various kinds of excommunication from the church. For that reason, most of us handle it as if it were a live hand grenade: we dare not lay it down, but we don't want to hang onto it either. I doubt that Christ intended anything like a doctrine of excommunication.

The first step is to confront the brother or sister in private, face to face. Step two reflects the truth that the body of Christ is in fact united by the Spirit of God. Those who might reject our initiative as "one person's opinion" may well reconsider when third parties intervene in love. Step three is simply the extension of the other steps. The church of God unites to pursue peace side by side with all people. If the other party still refuses to be reconciled, "treat him as you would a pagan or a tax collector."

How do obedient Christians treat tax collectors and pagans? Are we to ostracize them and avoid contact with them? Of course not. Jesus was roundly criticized because he had so much direct contact with tax collectors and (practical) pagans. We treat them as Jesus did: he loved them, built bridges to them where he could, treated them with kindness and consideration, prayed for them. But because their sin blocked the reciprocal fellowship he wanted to enjoy with them, he demanded no response.

When are we going to learn that we cannot make people do what they are supposed to do? Some Christians employ all kinds of pressure tactics to force other Christians into line. (You see it at times in Christian parents' relationships with their children.) But what do responsive believers do when their initiatives of peace fall on deaf ears or hard hearts? They release their opponents into the loving care of the Father. Yes, release them! Let them go! Demand nothing, expect nothing, but continue to love and give with no strings attached, as Jesus loved the tax collectors and gave himself to them.

Radical? You bet. Christlike? Right on. Effective? How will we ever know unless we test the power of of forgiveness, unless we learn to forgive as God has forgiven us?

> Let us join—'tis God commands—
> Let us join our hearts and hands;
> Help to gain our calling's hope,
> Build we each the other up:
> Still forget the things behind,
> Follow Christ in heart and mind,

Toward the mark unwearied press,
Seize the crown of righteousness.

While we walk with God in light,
God our hearts doth still unite;
Dearest fellowship we prove,
Fellowship in Jesus' love:
Sweetly each, with each combined,
In the bonds of duty joined,
Feels the cleansing blood applied,
Daily feels that Christ hath died.

Still, O Lord, our faith increase,
Cleanse from all unrighteousness:
Thee the unholy cannot see;
Make, O make us meet for thee!
Every vile affection kill,
Root out every seed of ill,
Utterly abolish sin,
Write thy law of love within.

Hence may all our actions flow,
Love the proof that Christ we know;
Mutual love the token be,
Lord, that we belong to thee:
Love, thine image, love impart!
Stamp it on our face and heart!
Only love to us be given!
Lord, we ask no other heaven.

Charles Wesley

NOTE

[1]Corrie ten Boom, *The Hiding Place* (Old Tappen, N.J.: Chosen Books, 1971), 215.

17

RUNNING THE RACE AND OVERCOMING FAILURE

Hebrews 12:15–17

A country fellow was caught red-handed by the sheriff with the neighbor's chickens in his sack. But the next Sunday he took his place in the choir as usual and sang as lustily as ever. In fact, he got so taken up in the service that he became shoutin' happy. The pastor confronted him after the service. "How can you steal chickens on Tuesday and shout on Sunday?" He responded, "But, Preacher, I ain't going to let a few chickens interfere with my religion!"

We are faced in evangelical Christianity with a scorching drought of basic Christian accountability. I include, with a grieving heart, examples from my own experience—with details disguised. The Reverend Thomas James—Brother Tom to his friends—came to Southwark Chapel after serving two congregations effectively. It was a momentous event for the folk at Southwark because Tom was to be the first full-time pastor in the twenty-year history of the congregation. He was a gifted preacher with so much charisma that strangers warmed to him quickly.

Within a year, however, Tom had skipped town, leaving his wife and four children without income or housing. Then the truth came out. In his previous church, he had had an affair with a member of the congregation. The conference superintendent stepped in to "try to protect Tom's ministry." He had extracted a promise from him that he would break off the relationship. The superintendent then arranged for him to transfer to Southwark Chapel. The immorality, however, was kept carefully covered.

The affair did not end. Tom picked up his woman and headed west. His ministry was destroyed. His family was devastated. His superintendent was discredited. Southwark Chapel was left reeling, ultimately losing a number of families in the storm of division and suspicion that paralyzed the ministry of the church.

Eric Stephenson was another pastor friend of mine. The great difference in our ages did not prevent our becoming good friends. I did not know what was going on in Eric's life at the time, though in hindsight I can see telltale markers. Unexplained absences, erratic behavior, conflict in the home all pointed toward serious problems. Perhaps I was too young and naïve to see them then, but other fellow pastors saw—and looked the other way. Eric was an alcoholic.

The conference solved the problems in Eric's parish by making him district superintendent! A few knew the whole story, but they kept quiet "to keep from hurting Eric." Years later Eric's marriage collapsed under the weight of accumulated conflict. The solution this time was to promote him to a denominational office. Eventually he left the ministry. He never did the damage that Tom did, except to himself and his own family. But both stories—and countless more like them—could have had happy endings, if we had been biblical Christians.

Eric had never taken his alcoholism lightly. I doubt that Tom ever took his affairs lightly either, but I don't know the details. Eric had fought his problem all his life. I imagine that he cried, prayed, suffered over it, maybe even fasted over it. I suspect he had asked God's forgiveness 10,000 times, each time begging for strength to resist. But the bottle always came back to haunt him, his family, and the church. For all his earnestness, Eric had gone back to drink again and again.

In these stories are two kinds of failure. These pastors who fell into sin had already failed long before the outward sin blasted their worlds to splinters. But fellow Christians aided and abetted their fall; pastor colleagues and denominational leaders all failed them.

THE PROBLEM OF ACCOUNTABILITY

In every well-managed business, each employee knows the superior to whom he or she answers. "You report to . . . " is part of every good job description. Accountability serves to focus the efforts and abilities of thousands of individuals— clerks, engineers, accountants, executives—to the pursuit of a single objective. Americans understand that. We expect to be held responsible for our performance on the job, we demand it of our employees, and we require our elected officials to answer for their actions, both personal and public.

But to discuss accountability in Christian living is another matter altogether. The idea instantly raises fearsome phantoms in our minds. Christians may be uncomfortable with the thought that God knows all about them anyway. But he is at least invisible—we don't have to look him in the eye Monday morning. But to think that a fellow believer should know something about our private lives is truly frightening.

As modern Christians, we are even more ill at ease with the other side of accountability—looking into the lives of Christian friends. Invading the privacy of another is perhaps the most awful social blunder that we can commit. Yet we are faced with an explicit command from our Hebrew author: "See to the spiritual and moral well-being of fellow Christians." What are we going to do about it?

WE ARE OUR BROTHERS' KEEPERS

Let's look closely at the particular problems we are to look out for. The passage has three phrases. "See to it that no one misses the grace of God." The verb *misses* means to "fall back from." It specifically points to those who have experienced the grace of God and then backed away. Already in this epistle the author has given us two stern warnings about falling away from God. Now he instructs us to pay attention to our brothers and sisters and to do all we can to prevent them from falling away. We are not commanded merely to notice that some fall away but to get involved to prevent them from falling away.

The sentence continues: "See to it . . . that no bitter root grows up to cause trouble and defile many." Bitterness and resentment are endemic in too many congregations. Where resentments are nursed, every act of evil is possible, and the love of God cannot survive. Certainly we are not commanded to read minds, but we are instructed to be watchful. How far would gossip go if we took this seriously? Imagine the shock if, when a friend complains, "Do you know what he did to me?" we would respond, "Have you forgiven him?"

There is one more. "See that no one is sexually immoral, or is godless like Esau." The two statements fit together. Esau was not sexually immoral (so far as we know). But he was guilty of selling his future for immediate gratification of his physical desires. Even though his immediate desire was food, not sex, thousands today are following his example in the sexual dimension of life. Most of the young couples who come to me for marriage are church attenders and professing Christians. Yet experience now compels me to ask whether they are living together or sexually involved. I feel like Rip Van Winkle as I try to convince them that they are selling their future for pleasure now.

Here, then, are three threats to God's work in our lives. The danger of hardening is a personal spiritual one. The danger of resentment is a threat to the fellowship of the church. And the danger of living for the present destroys the testimony of God's people in this world—that is the way the world lives, and we become like it. These three dangers don't comprise all possible dangers, but they do suggest to us that we are other believers' keepers.

ACCOUNTABILITY IS NOT A FISHING LICENSE

Part of our resistance to accountability is our very natural and reasonable fear of its misuse. As a result of our fallen condition, some—perhaps many—of us wrestle with what some psychologists call *a will to power*. The will to power is a perverted response to our human weakness. Because a man or woman is weak (like the rest of us, to be sure), he or she may choose to camouflage weakness. Two covers are immediately available: knowledge and influence.

People use knowledge to build themselves up and—often—to tear others down. Any scrap of information that undermines or belittles someone else is put to immediate use. We call these kinds of people *gossips*. We may find more of them in our churches than anywhere else because "Christian concern" gives such a respectable excuse for prying into others' lives. The threat of exposure is the most powerful argument I know of for keeping quiet about our secret and personal battles.

Three preachers were traveling by train some distance from the city in which they all served. Conversation turned to serious matters, and one suggested that since he had no one at home to whom he could tell his inner battles, this was a good opportunity for all of them to let down their hair and admit their weaknesses. The three agreed, and the first confessed a secret weakness for good wine. The second thought for a few seconds, then admitted that his weakness was R-rated movies. The third paused only a moment, and blurted out, "My greatest weakness is gossiping, and I can't wait to get off this train!" As we chuckle, we know why we fear accountability.

But the second cover is even more dangerous: influence. A host of otherwise Christian people feel called to control those about them. Using pressure, guilt, trickery, bribery, and many other tools, they set out to make others do what they want them to do. Authoritarian men, domineering women, entrenched church bosses, pastors who mount moral crusades against any who dare to disagree with them: all will use every opportunity to exert personal control over their colleagues.

Accountability can play directly into the hands of weak and defensive people. I came into contact with such extremes while in England several years ago. A strong house-church movement was underway there. In some of these groups accountability had become a tool of control. No personal decisions whatever could be made without consultation with an elder of the group, often termed a shepherd. Purchase of a car or home, taking a vacation, even family relationships had to be reviewed. Even worse, the decision of the elder was final, without recourse. God spoke through him. Both gossip and control are perversions of accountability.

Biblical accountability is unlike that of politics or the workplace. In the world, accountability moves (supposedly) up a scale of power or importance. In other words, if I make myself accountable to you, you become superior to me; I assume a lower rank. But biblical accountability flows only and always between equals. Paul made equality clear in Galatians 6:1–5. "If someone is caught in a sin, you who are spiritual should restore him gently." But then Paul warns about the dangers of feeling superior, of congratulating ourselves on our "higher" position. "If anyone thinks he is something when he is nothing, he deceives himself."

Again, the fellowship of God's people appears as companionship among weak and fallen people who need each other. The foundation of accountability lies in the understanding that we walk shoulder to shoulder with every other child of God. When a brother or sister confesses a weakness or failure or problem, I am humbled. Why, with my own collection of weaknesses and failures, would anyone trust me? What do I really have to offer? I know so little and my experience is so narrow. I can offer only what I have: love, acceptance, understanding—because I desperately need all these myself.

When I see a fellow Christian foundering, love compels me to reach across to him and offer my help. I reach *across* to him, not *down*. I have nothing to offer him (or her) except what I receive from God, and I offer that freely without strings. He may respond to my offer and be restored to fellowship with God. He may reject my hand and slip deeper into sin. But I gain no personal power when he responds, and I lose no face when he refuses. I cannot force him, just as my heavenly Father does not force me to respond.

It would take another book to explore all that it means to restore another who wanders or succumbs to resentment or slips into outward sin. But I want to turn our attention to what you and I must do now—the very first step to discovering the benefits of loving accountability with a fellow Christian.

STEPS TO BECOMING ACCOUNTABLE

We cannot make another believer become accountable to us. Biblical accountability cannot exist where there is no freedom. But we can make ourselves answerable to respected brothers and sisters. We can and we must.

The first two steps to accountability are familiar because we take these steps every time actions or attitudes strain our fellowship with God. First, we must be honest with ourselves about our weaknesses. That means that we lay aside excuses and explanations, and admit that there are areas of our lives that fall short. We stop throwing the blame toward others. We accept responsibility for our actions and attitudes.

The second step is honesty with God. We must confess our weaknesses and failures. We ask his forgiveness, and he grants it to us instantly and totally. But God intends to do more than forgive us; he is also sanctifying us. When we are honest with ourselves and with God, we can begin to understand how much God cares about our ingrained patterns of weakness and failure. All along he *has been sanctifying* us. In fact, the sense of weakness and failure is plain evidence that he is at work in our lives. When we are honest, we open the door for real healing.

If the confession of our weaknesses to God is not the end, what is the next step? James tells us, "Confess your sins to each other and pray for each other so that you may be healed" (5:16). Obviously, our companions do not forgive our sins. They may forgive us if we have harmed them, but they cannot forgive our sins. The purpose in this command is to bring us face to face with our pride.

How often Christians' response to that command is, "Who, me? You've got to be kidding! I will never tell another soul so long as I live!" But unless we obey, we will never have victory. Why? God is certainly able to give us directly and individually power to overcome anything. But our pride thwarts the sanctifying work of God because he has chosen to use his children to shape one another.

Pride causes our first question to be, "What will people think of me?" We assume that because we despise the weaknesses and sins we see in ourselves that others would automatically despise us if they knew. The fear of rejection is a well-founded fear, but it is only another barrier to healing and victory. We must swallow the pride. We have been honest with ourselves and with God; now we must be honest with other believers. Only when we take all three steps of honesty are we approaching the place where God can use us to restore a wandering brother. Jesus said it as simply as it can be said, "You hypocrite, first take the plank out of your own eye, and then you will see clearly to remove the speck from your brother's eye" (Matt. 7:5).

I don't understand it, but I know that it works. When we are willing to take our weaknesses seriously enough to ask for the help of other believers, the healing power of God comes to us. These brothers and sisters in whom we confide must be growing as Christians and demonstrating a spirit of loving Christlikeness. They must be Christians who pray, for we need constant prayer in this accountable fellowship. They must be strong and courageous enough to ask hard and probing questions and to hold us to the commitments we make with them before God.

Becoming accountable has been difficult for me because I have always been a closed person when it comes to my feelings and problems. As at other points in this book, I can here only point you in the direction I intend to travel. But I am learning. I first had to begin to be accountable to my wife. That meant telling her of my feelings and ideas, and giving her a veto over my plans. I was amazed at how much trouble she could save me from, if I would only open up and listen!

Then I began to open my personal affairs to my congregation's official board. Many pastors are not so blessed as I, but my board is composed of trustworthy men near my age, who both love me and are honest with me. I am learning to submit, without personal defensiveness, all my plans and ideas to their judgment and to learn from them. I value their responses and treat their questions, even the pointed ones, as expressions of loving concern.

Then there are the individuals. On one occasion I learned by way of the grapevine that several leaders had been offended by a statement I had made in a sermon. It was possibly the hardest thing I ever did, but I went to each of them and said point blank, "I understand that you are upset with me. I would like to hear it from you. What is wrong between us?" In each case, I learned something of how I appeared to my fellow Christians. The images were not entirely flattering, but the lessons were priceless.

There is much about my life that I still tell to no one. But I am far more open than I was even five years ago. Consequently, I am freer, more confident, more joyful. I am learning, perhaps more slowly than I should, that I have nothing to fear from living life God's way. If what I now enjoy in my relationship with God and his people is a taste of what he has for me in the future, I can hardly wait!

> Help us to help each other, Lord,
>   Each other's cross to bear,
> Let each his friendly aid afford,
>   And feel his brother's care.
>
> Help us to build each other up,
>   Our little stock improve;
> Increase our faith, confirm our hope,
>   And perfect us in love.
>
> Up into thee, our living Head,
>   Let us in all things grow,
> Till thou hast made us free indeed,
>   And spotless here below.
>   Charles Wesley

18

COMPANIONSHIP WITH CONSUMING FIRE

Hebrews 12:18–29

If we are to be eternally saved from sin, we must become companions of a holy God. If we are to walk in companionship with God, we must become like him. If we are to become like him, we must walk in fellowship with his church. All three steps depend on our response to the grace of God. It is because of his grace that he has revealed himself in creation, in Jesus, and in his Word: that is grace. Hearing is our response.

This passage is the climax of the epistle to the Hebrews. It contains the last of three great warnings that our author directed to the Hebrew Christian church. But before the warning is given, he paints with words a graphic contrast between those who refuse to listen and those who hear.

THE TERROR OF SINAI

This description of God—a God of fear and fire—comes directly from the book of Exodus. Moses had led the children of Israel through the Red Sea on their way to the Promised Land. Until Moses arrived from the wilderness, this nation had not known God except through legends from the distant past. Now Moses had led them to this mountain, Sinai, for a rendezvous with the I AM. God told him that he was going to come in a dense cloud to speak with him so that all the people would hear God's voice.

On the appointed day all the Israelites gathered around the base of that desolate mound of rock. Strict limits were established, and trespassers were threatened with instant death. Then God came down. The mountain began to tremble as though it were going to crumble into dust. Clouds of black smoke surrounded it, and lightning unlike anything humans had ever seen before laced the sky. Nature was in an awesome uproar, and amidst the rumbling and the thunder came an unearthly trumpet blast.

Then God spoke. His voice sounded like peals of thunder echoing down the barren valleys, yet the words were distinct. But the words brought no comfort; the people began to tremble with fear and to back away. They came to Moses and said, "Moses, you speak to us, but don't ever let God speak to us again. We might die."

Why were the people so terribly frightened by the voice of God? The physical phenomena were certainly daunting, but it was not until he spoke that terror really gripped them. Could it be that God deliberately staged this encounter to scare the people into obedience? If that was his intention, it didn't work because within a few weeks they were creating a golden calf to worship. Besides, the God revealed in the rest of the Bible does not control people by terrorizing them. Neither would God instill terror for his own pleasure, like a boy who sneaks up on his mother with a big "Boo" just to enjoy the effects.

If terror was not God's intention, then why were the people terrified? This brings us to the point that our writer wanted to make. God's method of dealing with us has always been, from the very beginning, to tell us the truth and give us an opportunity to respond. The terror here at Sinai was not the intention of God; it was Israel's response to the truth of God.

The Israelites had a problem relating to God. And so do we. In simplest terms, our problem is that God is holy and we aren't. These people had already seen God protect them. They had seen the plagues, the divided sea, the manna, and the cloud of fire. But at each encounter with the power of God, they had chosen to find fault and grumble.

Terror was the natural offspring of rebellion. God intended to extend an invitation to his people to join him in intimate companionship. But they had refused to hear those words. So the very words of peace struck chords of fear in their hearts. They had refused to become what God wanted to make of them so now they could not stand in his holy presence. The distance between us and our God is never so great as when he speaks and we refuse to listen. For those who refuse to hear, the future holds nothing but terror and disintegration.

THE JOY OF ZION

Our Hebrew brother quickly moves on to another picture to assure us that the choice to listen to God results in a radically different outcome (12:22–24). He does not describe a historical event like Mt. Sinai because the scene sketched here has never happened in any earthly place. But neither was our Hebrew brother merely drawing a picture of heaven, for he announces, "You have come"—present perfect tense. This scene reveals the present reality of God's spiritual family. Our author describes a great festival in which throngs come together in the praise and worship of God. It is a scene of thanksgiving, praise, and joy.

Note the list of participants in this celebration: jubilant angels, a radiant church, throngs of righteous men and women—and God, the judge of all. Should that not strike fear into the hearts of that assembly, at least the human hearts there? No! This glorious multitude can acknowledge the presence of the Judge—of their Judge—with songs of joy. Why? They had chosen to listen to him, to respond to his sanctifying work.

God intends for us to be like him. The plan that he ordained to accomplish that goal is outlined here in Hebrews 12. "Laying aside the entangling sin" begins the transformation by unifying divided hearts. Our Father's discipline so that "we may share in his holiness" advances that transformation step through painful step. The fellowship of the church, where weak believers are strengthened and all learn to be accountable to one another, aids the process by placing us in the company of others who are being transformed. Together we seek "the sanctification, without which no one will see the Lord."

The Hebrew church was in grave danger of discounting the preeminence of Jesus Christ. He was the Word of God, spoken in human form at this particular point in history. The problem was not that the old law and ordinances were wrong or bad. The whole of the Old Covenant was good for its limited purpose. But God had spoken again, and they could not go back to Sinai without refusing to listen to this fresh Word.

Apart from response to the Word of God in Jesus, the terrible side of God that the Israelites faced at Sinai is the only side of God that we fallen humans can ever see. The final judgment will be the scene at Sinai multiplied a million times over, as the unsaved cry for rocks and mountains to fall on them and hide them from the face of the One who sits on the throne.

In a subtle and sinister way we, too, are being tempted to discount the preeminence of Christ. We discount his work whenever we argue that obedient companionship with God is not essential to eternal salvation. To hear some explain it, believers do not have to be (or cannot be) holy since Christ was holy in our place and lived a sinless life. Believers don't even have to be obedient, and they can even repudiate their relationship with God by open sinfulness and yet be saved! But if there is one clear word that God gives us in this epistle—and in the Scriptures altogether—it is that *he intends to make us like himself*—starting now!

In a final, climactic warning, our Hebrew pastor urges, "See to it that you do not refuse him who speaks" (12:25). To refuse God's plan is to settle for no plan, no hope, no way out. But God's plan is itself disconcerting because God himself is disconcerting; for our "God is a consuming fire" (v 29).

One of our overworked evangelical axioms is that God hates sin but loves the sinner. That is probably the understatement of all time. But it is not that God hates sin as some of us hate pornography, violence, or shameless sitcoms. It is far deeper and more serious than that. God does not merely dislike sin; the truth is that God's very nature rejects sin, is repelled by sin.

Perhaps the writer had in the back of his mind the story of Nadab and Abihu in Leviticus 10. They were the sons of Aaron consecrated to serve as priests. They decided that they were going to do this business their way. God had given clear instructions: use only the fire on the altar that had issued from the Holy Place. Instead, these men took out their matches and lit the torch, and approached the altar with "strange fire."

The account states that fire came from the presence of God and destroyed them. It was not the fire from the altar, but fire from the presence of God—the inner sanctuary of the tabernacle. When sin comes into the presence of God, it is as if the nature of God explodes in judgment. It is his nature to repel sin, to repudiate evil. If we harbor sin, though we may cover it ever so carefully, we find ourselves confronted with consuming fire.

We cannot cleanse ourselves; in fact, we cannot even see ourselves as we actually are. We have no chance of escaping judgment except in listening to the voice of God as we walk the paths of life. He tells the truth. To those who listen, the door to companionship with God is opened. We walk safely with Consuming Fire.

> Talk with us, Lord, thyself reveal,
>   While here o'er earth we rove;
> Speak to our hearts, and let us feel
>   The kindling of thy love.
>
> With thee conversing, we forget
>   All time and toil and care;
> Labor is rest, and pain is sweet,
>   If thou, my God, art there.
>
> Thou callest me to seek thy face,
>   'Tis all I wish to seek;
> To hear the whispers of thy grace,
>   And hear thee inly speak.
>
>   Charles Wesley

19

IT'S TOUGH TO LEAD
(AND FOLLOW)

Hebrews 13:7–8, 17

American Christians are as much the heirs of the American democratic traditions as the rest of the population. We elect our officials and hold them accountable for their actions. And American congregations tend to treat their pastors in the same way. Some churches subject their pastors to annual votes of confidence; others hold their positions solely on the pleasure of a board of deacons or elders while still others are under the authority of an ecclesiastical hierarchy. But all pastors understand that what their people think of them really matters!

The writer of this epistle addressed these final exhortations—as he did the rest of the letter—to "lay" Christians, though the term as we use it would have been meaningless to first-century believers. They were all in "full-time Christian ministry." But some had been chosen as leaders, and our brother included a few words about the relationship between the leaders and those who were led. He instructed those who followed to remember their leaders, to imitate their faith, and to submit to their authority (13:17).

Two key words place the issue of biblical leadership in perspective. The writer commands the followers to *imitate* their leaders. What kind of leaders are worthy of imitation? He also commands them to *submit* to their leaders. What is that special kind of bond that links leaders with the brothers and sisters who follow in God's church?

LEADERS WORTHY OF IMITATION

Pastors are pressured by our cultural emphasis on the financial and statistical bottom line to adopt a political model of leadership rather than a biblical model. This is a disheartening situation. These comments on the differences between political and spiritual leadership arise from my own struggles.

In our political democracy, we voters cast our ballots for candidates who support policies that we believe will be good for our nation or for us personally. Every political leader knows that his job depends on pleasing his constituency. At the very least he must keep happy those who command votes or those who make lots of noise. The political arena is not a place conducive to nurturing leaders who put conscience ahead of popularity. In fact, I fear that too many voters will always vote against a candidate who tells unpleasant truth. But telling people only what they want to hear is not leadership.

The church of Jesus Christ is not a democracy or a republic. God did not institute a representative government nor does everyone get to vote. Christ is the sole sovereign and supreme authority in his church. He is King, Master, and Lord; and his word is law. In the church the people—the members— are not the final authority as they are in the political realm. It is God himself who is our authority. Biblical leadership looks to God, not to the congregation.

My church has a long tradition of annual pastoral votes: a former pastor served for thirty years and faced twenty-nine elections! As I ponder this strange, grotesque invention of modern Christianity, I am fascinated and appalled. We have mixed spiritual leadership, the call of God, and the trappings of political contests. That raises a disturbing question for me: how can I be accountable both to God, who called me to preach, and to the congregation that pays my salary? Do I curry the favor of my people or seek the mind of God?

Let me use a personal example to illustrate the conflict.

One of the unwritten expectations that most American churches place on their pastors is extensive visitation, and my congregation has been served by a series of pastors who called from breakfast to bedtime several days each week. The number of visits made is one of the scores we keep to measure the pastor's work. (Check the statistical pages in the annual report!)

The pastor is supposed to call on the sick, the hospitalized, the infirm, the aged, the absentees, the prospects, the neighbors around the church, the neighbors of the members, and, of course, each member two or three times a year. (I'm being somewhat facetious!) Generally, though, the pastor who gives extensive calling first priority in time and energy is well-liked and "successful." But many pastors I know are driven to visitation by the political realities—not the spiritual.

The temptation to sacrifice study time, prayer time, and thinking time is strong. To put it bluntly, they cheat on preaching to meet the expectations of the congregation. Yet the Scriptures make preaching the first priority. "Let the elders who rule well be considered worthy of double honor, especially those who work hard at preaching and teaching" (1 Tim. 5:17, NASB). But taking time to read and prepare as Paul commanded Timothy takes a big hunk out of time spent in calling.

The pressure that the expectations of the congregation place on the pastor are subtle but powerful. There are times that I feel guilty when I spend time in study, when I read a book, when I take a long walk to wrestle with the application of a passage of Scripture. This unseen pressure erodes my commitment to be the best teacher I can be. I must be constantly on guard. Erosion is a compromise; when I yield to the expectations of my people in this area, I fudge on my obedience to the commission God has given me.

There are many other areas of conflict that tempt the conscientious pastor to be a political leader: styles of preaching, emotion in public services, community involvement, denominational loyalty, missionary emphasis, counseling (that is my list—every pastor's is slightly different). In each area lurks subtle pressure to give people what they want or think that they need. But how does God look at the situation? Can I safely assume that my people's approval is God's approval as well?

My greatest trials in the ministry stem from the fact that I don't fit the stereotypes. I know that at the pastoral election, twenty or thirty or forty percent of my congregation judge me on the fact that I do not meet their expectations. That is pressure! Now, tell me how easy it is to be accountable to God! What if only half of my congregation judge me in that way?

So this is the choice that every leader must make. We can ignore the pressure and the expectations and press on to seek change, renewal, revival, and fresh applications of timeless Scripture. We can continue to demand that our people approach the Word with mind and heart open. That is biblical leadership. Or we can abandon, bit by bit, the unique gifts and priorities that God has given us, and conform to the expectations of others. That is political leadership.

The dilemma is agonizing. We need, as human beings, some measure of encouragement and approval from fellow believers. Without the approval of our congregations, we have no ministry at all. But if we succumb to the pressure to conform, we begin to die. Our dreams fade, our relationship with God begins to go stale. Spiritually and emotionally we begin to shrivel.

I have heard Paul's words from 2 Timothy 4:3–4 thrown at liberal churchmen and congregations: "The time will come when men will not put up with sound doctrine. Instead, to suit their own desires, they will gather around them a great number of teachers to say what their itching ears want to hear." But we evangelicals have our own set of myths; our churches bear few marks of the presence of God, and evangelical churches too often turn away from those who challenge the myths with fresh insights into God's Word.

The leaders that our Hebrew brother wanted his fellow believers to imitate were not politicians who tried to move with the tide of popular opinion. As different as James, Paul, Barnabas, and Peter were in personality and style, they shared one basic characteristic: they took their counsel from the Lord Jesus himself. Paul went to a great deal of trouble in the epistle to the Galatians to show that he had received directly from God the message he preached. He had the approval of the leaders of the church, but Paul had heard from the Lord!

Biblical leaders are a tough breed, but they are not authoritarian. Those who study management styles talk of the SNL—the strong, natural leader. One management consultant mentioned to me that strong, natural leaders, in the church or elsewhere, tend to build organizations that collapse when they step out of the picture. Such leaders naturally demand that things be done one way—their way. We often equate biblical leadership with an SNL style, and that is unfortunate.

Paul was probably an SNL type, but very early he learned that accountability to fellow Christians is essential. That lesson too few Christian leaders today have mastered. In this sense, accountability is nothing more than the old-fashioned work of listening. Biblical leaders find their goals and visions in the presence of God, but they work out those God-given dreams in the arena of personal relationships. It is one thing to hear directly from God. It is another to hear indirectly from him through companions and other Christians. No leader can wholly follow God without hearing him both ways.

Jesus warned his disciples that the world's models of leadership did not belong in the church: "You know that the rulers of the Gentiles lord it over them, and their high officials exercise authority over them. Not so with you. Instead, whoever wants to become great among you must be your servant" (Matt. 20:25–26). Servants listen and listen carefully. In this multifaceted web of relationships God calls his church, no man or woman can dare claim to have the final word on God's truth. Every brother and sister has something to contribute to us and our understanding of the will of God.

In a fallen world like this, much of what the leader hears must be discarded. Sister Smith always wants to run the pastor's affairs. Brother Bob usually begins with, "God told me . . . " and what follows sounds suspiciously like opinion dressed up in church clothes. Bushels of criticism and faultfinding are left at the leader's doorstep. But the leader who practices listening for the voice and wisdom of God will often be surprised at the channels God uses. This quality of openness is an essential characteristic of biblical leadership.

These two qualities, then, I want to see developing in the lives of those who follow (and imitate) me: the commitment to take their cues directly from God and the openness to hear him through fellow believers. This is not contradictory but complementary, another reflection of the relational nature of God. These leaders I hope to see do not stop to determine which way the wind is blowing before they step out and commit themselves to a cause. They will draw so near to their Companion through the Scriptures that they will begin to see the world through his eyes. Yet they will listen to the most humble believer and sometimes hear the voice of God.

FOLLOWERS WORTHY OF GODLY LEADERS

True biblical leadership is difficult, and the lack of biblical followers makes things worse. But being a biblical follower is tough, too. Our author wrote some unsettling words: "Obey your leaders and submit to their authority." It brings to our minds people like Jim Jones. He gained such control over the hearts of hundreds of Christians that he led them to their deaths in the jungles of South America.

It is interesting that the writer of Hebrews used this particular word translated *submit*. This is the only place in the New Testament where it appears. It is not the usual word for submission. When we yield to God, that is unconditional surrender. We submit, we lay down our lives and allow God to assume absolute authority. We follow him without question. But the word used here means "to yield and remain independent." It is a guarded submission in which we yield to authority, yet we stand responsible for our own actions.

Biblical submission to church authorities is a conditional submission. We follow others only as we see that they are following the Lord Jesus. We keep one eye on them and one eye on the Word of God. Our conditional submission is essential for the work of the ministry because all human organization requires some kind of authority structure. Every group needs a measure of submission if it is to function as a body and work toward common goals. In any group, no individual has his or her own way all of the time. The values we share are so important that we gladly lay down personal opinions and preferences and submit to those who lead.

Conditional submission in the church is essential to biblical relationships. We in modern America should study again what is involved in being a congregation of believers. The church is the body of Christ composed of those who are saved individually by the grace of God. God's grace is free and impartial so no member has any claim to special knowledge of or special communication with God. God is free to speak or work through whomever he chooses.

Because the church is a body of interrelated believers, God never speaks to one member alone about his will for the group. He always speaks to several believers (sometimes one at a time), leading them in the same direction until their shared insights merged into a common understanding of God's will. If a congregation were composed of members who were all growing and maturing, unanimous decisions would be routine. The insight of each member would be one aspect of the revelation of God's will. Once such a consensus is created by the Holy Spirit, the church could act as a single organism with each member carrying part of the responsibility joyfully.

Such unanimity is all too rare, and I suspect that there will always be enough tares in the wheat to give God's leaders prematurely grey hair. Willful as too many of us are, submission will never be automatic. To make matters worse, submission has been more often demanded than nurtured, and the word has negative emotional connotations for most Christians. But Christian leaders can deliberately create a climate where conditional submission is easier than we might expect.

The willingness to share feelings and insights with leaders should be encouraged. As leaders we can seek out key people who think and pray, and ask for their opinions and insights. We can gently confront members who are unhappy and learn from their criticisms. Roundtable discussions with members of official boards, Sunday school teachers, parents of youth fellowship members, and small groups of members with common interests are gold mines of insight. Suggestion or comment boxes offer to timid souls opportunity for expression. The possibilities for input are limited only by our imaginations—when once we take the risk of seeking it.

A second way to encourage conditional submission involves opening ourselves as leaders to the prayer support of those who follow us. This is more than the casual "pray for me," and it can take many forms. John Maxwell, at the large Skyline Wesleyan Church of San Diego, enters the sanctuary with two laymen at the beginning of each service. The laymen pray for the pastor as the three kneel together at the communion rail. Charles Swindoll has a group of laymen who form a prayer group and meet weekly with him.

I have found that when I have honestly expressed to a small groups of believers my need for prayer, the subsequent support of these friends has strengthened my ministry—and theirs. It is so easy for leaders to build a facade of spiritual strength and superspirituality. The front is hypocrisy, of course, yet a convenient way to hide our own weaknesses. But God forbid that those who follow me should imitate my hypocrisy! If those who follow me must imitate me (and they will), I want to give them a model of open, honest, sanctified humanity. Only God knows how badly our world needs real Christians!

> Except the Lord conduct the plan,
> The best concerted schemes are vain
> And never can succeed:
> We spend our wretched strength for naught,
> But if our works in thee be wrought,
> They shall be blest indeed.
>
> In Jesus' name behold we meet,
> Far from an evil world retreat
> And all its frantic ways;
> One only thing resolved to know
> And square our useful lives below,
> By reason and by grace.
>
> Charles Wesley

20

LIVING OUTSIDE THE CAMP

Hebrews 13:7–16

The highest, holiest day in the Jewish religious year was the Day of Atonement. It was the tenth day of the seventh month, corresponding approximately to October. The sense of solemn importance was emphasized by the fact that this was the only day of the year that any person could enter the inner chamber of the temple. That person could be only the high priest, and he went through an elaborate ritual before entering that sacred precinct where God dwelt between the cherubim. Leviticus 16 describes this day.

The central ritual was the sacrifice of the great sin offering. In addition to the sacrificial bull, two male goats without defect were brought before the high priest at the door of the temple. One was chosen by lot, and the high priest slaughtered it. The blood was then carried into the Holy Place as an atonement for the sins of the whole nation.

Once the cleansing atonement had been completed, the high priest placed his hands on the head of the other goat, and confessed over that animal the sins of the people. The living goat was taken outside the camp and driven off into the wilderness to signify the removal of the people's sins. Finally, the carcass of the first goat (with other offerings) was taken outside the camp and burned as an offering for sin.

For centuries that pageant of the forgiveness and removal

of sin was repeated. It was enacted again in the mind of our Hebrew author as he wrote, "Jesus also suffered outside the city gate to make the people holy [*sanctify* in NASB] through his own blood" (13:12). But before we can follow him there, we must grasp the truth that he does not change.

Scripture is the lifeline of the believer. God did not reveal himself in theological arguments or philosophical proofs. He revealed himself in history. By far the largest part of the Bible is composed of accounts of God's work in the lives of men and women like us. They lived in a different time and a different age, dressed differently and talked different languages, but they were far more like us than they were different from us.

God met them in countless ways: in sorrow, hunger, sickness, persecution, death, and poverty. And Jesus Christ is the same yesterday, today, and forever (13:8). Whatever he has done for others, he is able to do for us. What he has done for us in the past he will do for us in the future, only more. How much less complicated our lives would be, and how much more joyful we would be, if we could grasp that truth in all its fullness. Jesus does not change. This affirmation holds several important implications for us today.

LIVING ON THE OUTSIDE WITH JESUS

Because Jesus is unchanging, he is central to believers' lives. He is our security, our anchor, our foundation, the only place we can stand with certainty in the tides of this world. He does not have to keep up with the times; Jesus stands outside and above the times. He is greater than the times. While everything is changing here on earth, flopping back and forth amid chaos, Jesus stands beyond time.

At precisely this point, we face one awful truth about this world and our relationship with it. Jesus is—must be—central to us who believe, but he is not important to this world. Our society has nothing to do with him and has no interest in him. The world banished him to a lonely cross outside the walls of Jerusalem and left him hanging with two criminals, facing the mockery of those who passed and watched. They wanted him dead and buried—permanently. The world has always treated Jesus that way and always will because human beings seek only their own way.

Jesus suffered outside the city gate. The people who made the decisions sat in the council chambers while Jesus walked toward Calvary. Those who had money and wealth were seated at their accounting tables while Jesus suffered. The social leaders, the influential, conducted their traditional religious celebrations while Jesus hung on the cross.

Forgetting that Jesus was left on the outside, the Christian church has tried from time to time to take its place in the seat of power. The Christian faith permeated the Roman Empire before it became a legal religion and ultimately the official faith. Yet in conquering the empire, the church nearly lost its soul. Standards for membership sagged under the weight of partially converted Romans (and, later, barbarians). The role of the emperor as umpire in quarrels about faith and worship opened the door wide for political abuses that made a mockery of Christian holiness.

The English Free Churches fell into the same trap at the end of the nineteenth century. Growing social influence gave Nonconformists the impression that political power was theirs for the taking. Yet at the point where it seemed that the Free Churches would unseat Anglicanism as the dominant faith of Britain, the movement fell apart. Their historic commitment to disciplined fellowship, personal spirituality, and uncompromising public witness against social evil had been watered down to make the churches more appealing. Nonconformists had lost their sense of mission as they sought the reins of power.

American evangelicals totter on the brink of the same precipice. It is not so much the power of the political right nor the influence of evangelical action groups in the formation of public policy. There is nothing wrong with political involvement; we are obligated by the command of Christ to do all the good that we can for our fellow citizens.

But our great danger lies in local congregations. Two generations ago we relaxed our discipline to receive more members under more lenient standards. We are heavily tainted with an insidious version of the prosperity gospel, which preaches that the American Dream is a promise from God of material wealth. It seems as though most evangelicals have unconsciously swallowed the secular idea that faith is a purely private matter not to be mentioned in private conversation. We still say the right words, but the conviction has ebbed out of them.

In seeking to be good citizens and faithful stewards—the salt of the earth—we can never forget that we don't fit here. We don't belong here. Many more would respond to the invitation of God if we could guarantee that those who walk with him would enjoy wealth and power and status. But history and our own experience prove to us what our Hebrew brother here declares: "Let us, then, go to him outside the camp, bearing the disgrace he bore." But when we go to him, not only do we discover the treasure of his presence, we find the companionship of his people.

FELLOW BELIEVERS ON THE OUTSIDE

Christian faith is an experience, not a creed. What we believe about God (our creed) is important because our beliefs determine our goals. We humans will seek what we believe is at least distantly possible, but we quickly tire when the goal is unattainable. Scripture, however, teaches us that God is seeking to become the Companion of obedient and responsive believers. And believe me, if any experience is worth writing home about, it is that of friendship with God!

I grew up among Christians who believed strongly in the importance of public testimonies about our experiences with God. I remember vividly those long prayer services around the Communion rail following revival meetings. Always we encouraged those who had come in response to the preaching to give some kind of public witness afterwards. It must have been a frightening prospect for the more timid, but it certainly made a point: we should tell others about our experiences with God.

I remain convinced to this day that the public witness of experience with God is an essential part of the fellowship of the church. When we encourage such sharing in public services or small groups, we open doors to a special ministry of the Holy Spirit. Not only do believers themselves gain when they share their personal encounters with God, the whole fellowship benefits in many ways. There is encouragement in words of experience; there is hope; there is insight and understanding.

I know that canned testimonies (I heard many, many of these as a child) are worse than meaningless; they are deadening. One of the perennial complaints about the old Methodist class and band meetings was that the same people used the same memorized and stylized "testimonies" week after week for years on end. Human laziness and spiritual stagnation will always be a problem in the church. But living accounts of daily encounters with the grace of God are priceless for the church.

"Remember those who led you," our Hebrew friend writes. To remember those who have gone before is to remember what God has done. When we think about what God did for others in the past, we often need to be reminded, as our writer goes on to remind us, that "Jesus Christ is the same yesterday and today and forever." Those who remember and imitate their leaders also remind one another of the work of God. When we join the company of those outside the gate, we find human relationships that are deep and enduring.

LEARNING TO ENJOY BEING AN OUTSIDER

In my eighth-grade year we were "initiated" into high school. As the preacher's son and a recent arrival in the community, I felt keenly that I was on the outside looking in, and anything the least embarrassing made it worse. All of the pranks were harmless enough though appropriately humiliating. But one really got to me. Eighth-grade boys were required to wear lipstick one day. I didn't like the idea at all. But the real rub was the fact that my conservative church took a strong stand against all makeup! I was not about to ask for a tube of red lipstick so I got around the requirement by pleading, "My church won't let me do that!"

And it was the same with school dances, outings, parties,

even friends. I knew I could never be a part of the in-group because of the standards my family held. At times I felt safety within those restrictions; at times I resented them. But they were there, astride one of the paths I could have chosen to take.

One vivid memory carries me back to the time when I returned to graduate school, now married with children. I worked part time and my employer threw a big Christmas party for all of us at a swanky local restaurant. We went, feeling very much on the outside, and he met my wife and me at the door with tickets for the bar. In a condescending voice loud enough to be heard across the room, he informed us that we could use our tickets to get Cokes! I had no desire to buy a martini; I wasn't even tempted. But why did he have to make an issue of our "outsider-ness"?

It seems sometimes that we believers are isolated and peculiar while the world is having a good time. But at long last I am beginning to view my place on the outside from a different perspective. If we step back and look at things from God's point of view, the outside becomes the inside! Jesus Christ never changes, but this world is disintegrating before our eyes. This world that seems so exciting, offering so much, is continually falling to pieces. People around us are working to accumulate possessions and power, only to discover that sooner or later everything crumbles into dust.

I never went to a circus or a fair that I can remember until after I was a teenager. That didn't bother me, but the fact that I had never had cotton candy did. When I got the chance, I went to a circus—just to get the cotton candy. I bought the biggest cone sold. I bit in—I was really going to enjoy it. But there was nothing there! I was distinctly disappointed! This nation is filled with people who are furiously eating cotton candy, and finding nothing there. They are the in-group!

The truth is this: all that is permanent is outside the city gate. This world has things all turned around. We have our backs turned to reality whenever we believers stand outside looking in, thinking how much easier it would be—how much more we could accomplish—if we were inside. This world is not permanent; its reality is a passing illusion.

One last time our writer brings us to face the word *sanctify*. "Therefore Jesus also that He might sanctify the people through his own blood, suffered outside the gate" (13:12, NASB). The NIV translates it, "make the people holy." We might have expected the writer to say that Jesus suffered outside the camp to justify or save us. That is true. But in this particular setting the writer is looking at a broader picture. Jesus died outside the camp to deliver us from the shackles that bind us to this disintegrating world. As fallen men and women we are bound mind and spirit to this world, which is disintegrating before our eyes. And had not Jesus suffered outside the gate, we would have disintegrated along with the world.

Appearances are never so deceiving as when we wonder about who is on the inside and who is on the outside. Everything in this world conditions us to look at appearances. We spend lots of money on clothes, cosmetics, diets, homes, cars, and plastic surgery. Success manuals teach that it is not nearly so important what you know as how you say what you know (or bluff when you don't know). The yuppie culture is based on the power of appearances to put people on the inside.

In our churches we have settled for appearances as well. Public professions of faith substitute for living, growing relationships with Jesus Christ. Faithful attendance and support replace discipleship. Classy entertainment takes the place of worship in spirit and truth. Tithing preempts a selfless commitment to be stewards of all God's blessings. We believe that activity is a sign that we are Christians, yet our hearts are cold.

Appearances are superficial. But the sanctifying work of God starts on the inside. He doesn't begin by remodeling our looks but our attitudes. What happens inside when we are criticized? Men and women of this world grow hostile and defensive, lose their tempers and strike out. When God is sanctifying us, he gives us the power to face the rising anger with a soft and gentle word.

What happens when we don't get our way, when others interfere with what we are trying to do? Men and women of this world fight, grow angry, scheme, plot, and conspire to get around those who oppose them. Or they walk off spewing bitter contempt all around them. But the Holy Spirit is teaching and enabling those who are being sanctified to accept opposition, to learn from those who oppose them, and even to love those who are their enemies.

What happens when we are treated unfairly, when someone takes advantage of us? Some men and women of this world angrily scheme to get even, trying to make those who cause suffering to suffer themselves. Others hold a pity party, inviting all who will listen to feel sorry for them. But when God is sanctifying us, we have the power to turn the other cheek, to go the second mile, to give and demand nothing in return. The sanctifying work of God makes us different. He is freeing us from this disintegrating world's shackles of greed.

It is really not so bad after all, being on the outside. I'm learning to enjoy it. I hope—O God, deliver me!—I hope that I never become patronizing or condescending toward the insiders of this world. But I relish the possibilities on the outside: companionship with an eternal, unchanging Savior and Lord, who is even at this moment transforming me into a better, more loving, more sensitive, more holy person. Perhaps someday I can learn to wear the reproach of Christ as a garment of rejoicing!

> Lord, we have come to thee
> In answer to thy call,
> And now, from sin set free,
> We gladly yield thee all.
>
> Lord, keep us unashamed
> In standing up for thee;
> Help us to bear the cross,
> And witness manfully.
>
> Edward H. Gladstone Sargent[1]

NOTE

[1] This hymn is used with the permission of the publisher and is taken from *Hymns of Faith and Life* (Indianapolis: Wesley Press, 1976), no. 297.

21

THE GREAT SHEPHERD OF THE SHEEP

Hebrews 13:20–21

I have always thought that sheep were docile, pleasant, usually obedient animals who didn't do anything but eat grass and grow wool. I have never been around sheep so I thought that when God calls us his sheep, he intended some sort of low-key compliment. Was I mistaken!

This passage is one of the reverent, classic benedictions of the Bible. It is also the first—and only—reference in the epistle to Jesus as Shepherd. I have had much to say about our responsiblity to respond to the grace of God poured so generously into our lives from day to day. But I have said much less than many would want me to say about the breadth and depth and power of the grace God gives.

JESUS IS THE GREAT SHEPHERD

It is significant that in the conclusion to this stirring epistle, Jesus carries the title of Shepherd. To understand something of the pervasiveness and power of the grace of God, take a look at the work of a conscientious shepherd. One worth his salt certainly has his hands full. Sheep are a pain![1]

First, sheep are creatures of blindly narrow habit. Sheep will walk in one path and one only, back and forth, until they turn it into a gully. They will graze the same plot over and over again until they actually eat the roots of the grass out of the ground. They will lie down in the same bedding ground under the same tree day after day, regardless of how many other shady spots there may be. The bedding area will become infested with parasites and vermin, but the sheep continue to return, even when infestations of insects drive them almost insane.

One of the prime responsibilities of the shepherd is to push or lead them into new grazing and bedding territory. That is just like our Shepherd! The Lord Jesus is constantly guiding us, prodding us, leading us out into new territory, new pastures, new watering places, new resting places. At times it seems that he almost drags us, kicking and struggling out of the old into the new, without our thanks or appreciation!

Second, an adult sheep, especially a healthy sheep with a heavy fleece of quality wool, is extremely dependent on the constant watchfulness of the shepherd. If a healthy sheep were accidentally to roll over on its back, it could not right itself. If it should lie there more than two or three hours, it would probably die. In panic it would thrash its legs in the air, but this exhausting effort is futile.

The careful shepherd frequently scans the pastures during daylight hours to look for any flailing feet in the air. Our shepherd knows, far better than the wisest of us, how desperately we need his watchfulness. At our best and strongest, we are but a single misstep from helplessness. Sheep have little to be arrogant about and so very much to be grateful for.

Third, sheep are quarrelsome. I was surprised. I had always thought that sheep were well-behaved! In every established flock is a butting order. At the head of the flock reigns an arrogant old ewe, and she can butt anyone she pleases, lie down wherever she chooses, and generally lord it over the flock. At the bottom of the hierarchy cowers a scrawny little runt that dares not butt anybody. He is the only one that has any peace, however, because he doesn't have to defend his position. Sheep left to themselves will be constantly quarreling, challenging each other's place in the butting order while each defends his own. None will lie down and rest.

When the shepherd notes the agitation, all he has to do is

walk into the field and the quarreling stops. The sheep will find themselves places to rest and chew their cuds. I have watched— and felt—petty bickering and self-interested competition evaporate when Jesus imparts to his church a special sense of his presence. And how urgently the melting, healing, cleansing breath of God is needed in our church today! Oh, that he would walk among us and lift our eyes from ourselves!

Fourth, sheep are among the most defenseless animals on earth. They cannot deal effectively with either petty irritations or mortal enemies. Flies and gnats are a constant source of discomfort. Unlike cattle they have no tails, and unlike dogs and cats they lack the ability to scratch themselves. Several types of flies congregate on a sheep's face and even lay eggs in its nostrils. Sheep will literally fret themselves to utter exhaustion trying to escape the flies.

The shepherd's care is essential to the health of the sheep. He regularly anoints the heads of his flock with repellents to control the insects and keep eyes and noses clear. It is the work of a patient, loving shepherd who feels the frustrations of his flock. It may be that the big threats (wolves and lions) are easier to identify and handle than the petty problems. We turn to God when we face the big issues, then allow the minor irritations of life to stifle our joy and erode our peace. But Jesus is concerned about anything that burdens or disturbs us.

Finally, sheep are timid. Their only means of defense is flight, and they can't run very fast. Nearly any dog can outrun a sheep, not to mention a cougar or lion. Sheep are, therefore, timid and easily frightened. A flock will panic and stampede at even a minor surprise. It is the work of the shepherd to be the eyes and ears of the flock, to see farther than the sheep can. The shepherd seeks to intercept the surprises and shocks, to prepare for them, to calm the flock with his presence because he wants his sheep to have peace and rest.

JESUS IS THE BEGINNING AND THE END

God's grace has no limits. It is his nature to pour upon creation an inexhaustible tide of loving, gracious, enablement.

"In him we live, and move, and have our being," Paul reminded the puzzled intellectuals in Athens (Acts 17:28). I have tried in this book to unwrap layer by layer the understandings that motivated our Hebrew author. The keystone of this epistle is the profound truth that our gracious God does not overpower us. He could. He certainly has the power and the right to impose his will throughout all creation. But he will not violate or withdraw the gift of the independent will he granted to Adam and his offspring.

Yet he does not leave us to fend for ourselves, wounded and terribly handicapped by our fallen nature. We will never comprehend the depth of the grace of God nor the lengths to which God goes to win to himself each fallen individual. Our writer wrapped up this flood of grace in three phrases in his benedictory conclusion. The first is "equip you with everything good." The second is "for doing his will." The third is "and may he work in us what is pleasing to him."

The verb translated equip (*perfect* in the KJV) is not the common word that Paul and other New Testament writers used for *maturity*. The word used here means "to adjust or to fit, to make up for a lack, to complete." In the ancient world it was a medical term, used when a doctor set a dislocated joint. It embodies the idea of putting things back the way they are supposed to be. That is a most appropriate description of the work of the Holy Spirit in believers' lives.

The dislocations of our human personalities center in our wills. An independent will is the gift of God; a rebellious will is a tragic dislocation. But God will not forcibly set things right. God loves without controlling, and he showers grace without demanding response. He seeks to equip us—set us right—by arranging the circumstances of life to lead us into his presence.

Yet I see so many people, and many professing Christians, fuming at their circumstances. They complain and fuss, angry over adversity. They make life difficult for themselves and everyone around. Yet they do not realize that it is the hand of the Shepherd in the circumstances. He is using them—all these difficulties that we want to escape—to complete them.

Gamaliel advised the Sanhedrin to proceed cautiously

against those troublesome believers in Jesus. If this movement was of human origin, he warned, it would collapse of itself, as other fads in the past had done. But if it was of God (as impossible as that must have seemed to these enemies of Jesus), they could not overcome it. "You will only find yourselves fighting against God" (Acts 5:39). When we rebel against our circumstances, we are in fact fighting against the hand of God who is trying to make us all he created us to be.

The second phrase is "for doing his will." Our Hebrew writer places great stress on the fact that we have real responsibility and make real choices. Had God wanted robots to carry out his desires unquestioningly, he would have created us robots. But he sought companionship with beings whom he created in his own image. That gift of an independent will is reflected in all of God's dealings with us. Every choice has its consequences, and in allowing us the freedom to make those choices, he also allows us the freedom to reap what we have sown. That miracle of enabling grace is the opportunity he gives us to choose to do his will.

The choice to do his will is ours, but the strength to do his will is his. The grace of God is always flowing toward us. Through grace—and grace alone—we are enabled to do what we have chosen to do, to do his will. This is the meaning of the final phrase: "may he work in us what is pleasing to him." All of the resources needed, all of the ability required, all of the understanding demanded flows only from God himself. His grace is his enabling power that transforms our choices into changed lives.

We can compare these three phrases to the beginning, the middle, and the end of a story. Every story has a beginning, a body, and an ending. God is the beginning of our story. Everything that is worthwhile and happy in our lives, every blessing, has its origin in Jesus Christ. And he is also the end of our story. Our best is never enough, never complete, never even remotely close to matching the need of the hour or the perfection of God.

God is working in us those things that are pleasing to him—he is pouring into us his grace, and he will continue to pour on his grace as long as we live here. As we respond, we will grow more like him day by day from the moment we accept Jesus as our Savior to the end of our lives. This is the sanctifying work of the Father. He leads us to the cross, and in response, we repent of our sins. Then he leads us to the Upper Room, where we respond by surrendering to his control our lives, our plans, our goals, our ambitions, our wills.

What about the middle of the story? We can choose to do the will of God, responding step by step to the initiatives of grace.

> Christ, our King before creation,
> Son, who shared the Father's plan,
> Crowned in deep humiliation
> By your friend and partner, man:
> Make us humble in believing,
> And, believing, bold to pray—
> "Lord, forgive our self-deceiving,
> Come and reign in us today!"
>
> Lord of life and Lord of history,
> Giving us, when man despairs,
> Faith to wrestle with the mystery
> Of a God who loves and cares:
> Make us humble in believing,
> And, believing, bold to pray—
> "Lord, by grace beyond conceiving,
> Come and reign in us today!"
>
> Word that ends our long debating,
> Word of God that sets us free,
> Through your body re-creating
> Man as he is meant to be:
> Make us humble in believing,
> And, believing, bold to pray—
> "Lord, in us your aim achieving,
> Come and reign in us today!"
>
> Ivor H. Jones

NOTE

[1]I am indebted to Phillip W. Keller's *A Shepherd Looks at Psalm 23* (Grand Rapids: Zondervan, 1970) for teaching me so much about sheep.